CW00688360

THE
DRIVING
INSTRUCTOR'S
GUIDE TO
TEACHING
THE THEORY

TEST

To Ann, with love.

THE
DRIVING
INSTRUCTOR'S
GUIDE TO
TEACHING
THE THEORY

TEST

**Endorsed by The
Motor Schools Association**

EDWARD BAKER

**KOGAN
PAGE**

YOURS TO HAVE AND TO HOLD

BUT NOT TO COPY

The publication you are reading is protected by copyright law. This means that the publisher could take you and your employer to court and claim heavy legal damages if you make unauthorised photocopies from these pages. Photocopying copyright material without permission is no different from stealing a magazine from a newsagent, only it doesn't seem like theft.

The Copyright Licensing Agency (CLA) is an organisation which issues licences to bring photocopying within the law. It has designed licensing services to cover all kinds of special needs in business, education and government.

If you take photocopies from books, magazines and periodicals at work your employer should be licensed with CLA. Make sure you are protected by a photocopying licence.

The Copyright Licensing Agency Limited, 90 Tottenham Court Road, London, W1P 0LP. Tel: 0171 436 5931. Fax: 0171 436 3986.

First published in 1996

Apart from any fair dealing for the purposes of research or private study, or criticism or review, as permitted under the Copyright, Designs and Patents Act, 1988, this publication may only be reproduced, stored or transmitted, in any form or by any means, with the prior permission in writing of the publishers, or in the case of reprographic reproduction in accordance with the terms and licences issued by the CLA. Enquiries concerning reproduction outside those terms should be sent to the publishers at the undermentioned address.

Kogan Page Limited
120 Pentonville Road
London N1 9JN

© Edward Baker, 1996

The right of Edward Baker to be identified as author of this work has been asserted by him in accordance with the Copyright, Designs and Patents Act 1988.

British Library Cataloguing in Publication Data

A CIP record for this book is available from the British Library.

ISBN 0 7494 1933 4

Typeset by Northern Phototypesetting Co Ltd, Bolton
Printed in England by Clays Ltd, St Ives plc

Contents

Contents

Foreword

The book you are holding is a practical, down-to-earth guide for the Approved Driving Instructor (ADI) who wants to offer theory training but who has little or no experience in this field. It is not a substitute for more formal training such as that offered by the City & Guilds course for dealing with adult learners, nor does it pretend to be the last word on the subject. What it will provide, however, is a solid foundation in theory training from start to finish – from assessment and lesson-planning to marking, from getting the most out of audio-visual equipment to dealing with demotivated or disruptive pupils. The ADI who reads and puts into practice the techniques in this manual will be more than able to deliver high-quality theory training.

Because this is also a selling situation in which the ADI faces external competition for the first time, it is recommended that you consult this book's companion volume – *The Driving Instructor's Guide To Effective Selling Skills*. Before you can teach, you must first sell.

1
THE IMPLICATIONS OF THE THEORY TEST

THE NEED FOR THE THEORY TEST

The facts of life and death are these. Each and every year in the UK thousands of people are maimed, crippled or killed by needless and preventable road accidents – accidents caused by inattention to the most basic of rules; accidents caused by speeding in poor weather conditions; accidents caused by the improper use of alcohol; accidents caused by dangers that learner drivers are warned about from day one of their training.

Of the above-mentioned casualties, a disproportionate number occur within the 17- to 25-year-old age group. The reasons behind this grim statistic are not that hard to understand. Youthful over-confidence, peer pressure, exuberance and the feeling of immortality that young people have, all of these and more contribute to the tragic news of road accidents that we see on television or read about in newspaper headlines. There is, however, a more serious problem that springs from the general public's attitude towards driving. The ability to drive is seen by far too many people in terms of status rather than as an on-going process. We commonly say 'Oh, he (or she) has passed their test', as though that is the end of it, an achievement that will never change or deteriorate. Once a driver has gained a full driving licence, 'experience' is supposed to take care of everything from judgement to good manners. Experience is, indeed, a fine and worthy teacher, but in a situation where a new driver takes a test in optimum conditions and then legitimately drives home in the dark on a motorway, the gaining of experience can be a hit-or-miss affair in every sense of the phrase!

In an effort to reduce road accident statistics, the Government has introduced a series of new measures, among which is the Theory Test. As of July 1996, all aspiring drivers will have to pass a short theory paper prior to their practical test, a move, incidentally, which will bring Britain into line with the rest of the European Community. The implications of this are profound for everyone concerned.

THE IMPLICATIONS FOR THE PUPIL

Few learner drivers will see the Theory Test as beneficial. Most will perceive it as another hurdle, another obstacle to prevent them from driving. It is, by definition, a test, bringing with it extra cost, nerves and the fear of failure. As driving is seen as a manual, practical skill, it will also bring frustration for those who are afraid of studying. No longer will a smattering of responses and a quick look at the Highway Code suffice. The learner driver must become a real student.

The net result of all this will be to act as a brake on the learner driver's progress. Like any other brake, though, it just might conceivably save a life. And, handled correctly, it could set a pattern for future learning in which driving skills are seen as life skills that need attention and the occasional overhaul.

THE IMPLICATIONS FOR THE ADI

The very fact that you are reading this book signals that you recognise the importance of the Theory Test in your working life as an Approved Driving Instructor. It is still worth pausing, however, to look at the consequences of *not* taking part in this process. The ADI who steps aside from this role runs the risk of:

1. Losing a huge market slice.
2. Losing credibility.
3. Losing a valuable new source of income.
4. Losing a new source of leads.
5. Losing the chance to develop life skills among pupils.

Each of these vital issues will now be explored in turn, in case you need further convincing!

Losing a market

The learner driver now has to begin the licensing process by first passing the Theory Test. In practical terms, this means that pupils will gravitate to those ADIs who offer theory tuition prior to, or alongside, practical lessons. You may argue that you will leave the dull and demanding aspects of teaching theory to another instructor and simply concentrate on driving lessons – but how likely is that to happen? If a pupil has selected and bonded with an ADI who can address their entire training needs, are they likely to approach you much before their third test attempt? The only completely new pupils that you will get will be those who have passed the Theory Test by themselves – and these will be very keenly fought over and not above abandoning you if you are not a first-class teacher!

You will also cut yourself off from learner drivers who want comprehensive tuition regardless of cost, such as those paid for by doting grandparents or companies, not to mention the fast-growing under-17s market. If you can afford to lose all of the above, then stop reading now and count the fortune you obviously have.

Losing credibility

Any ADI who does not offer a theory training package of some sort runs the risk of being thought old-fashioned or substandard. The lack of such provision will make pupils think that you are less capable than the opposition and presents them with a weakness to aim at!

Losing income

The loss of a valuable new source of income should concern any ADI, but teaching the Theory Test goes much further than just having a bit of extra cash. Those ADIs who construct a full training programme have created a contingency against bad weather or incapacity caused by, say, a broken arm. More to the point, the extra revenue allows for lesson subsidy or 'freebies' at a later stage. With a little imagination, you can come up with a competitive package that is hard to resist.

Losing leads

The ADI who adopts a centre-based method of tuition will find that the class acts as a social magnet. Not only will learner drivers bring along friends who want help with theory, they will also introduce others with practical driving difficulties.

Losing the chance to teach life skills

This is perhaps the most serious consequence of non-involvement with theory training. As mentioned earlier, there is a desperate need for driving skills to be seen as part of a life-long process rather than just a 'knack' developed for a 30-minute test. If the theoretical aspects of driving are left at this level, they will be forgotten like schoolday algebra, French, and so on.

Tomorrow's driver must feel the need for the constant updating and practice of skills. A regular check-up with an ADI must become as normal a part of existence as a visit to the doctor or dentist. This is a selling problem as much as a teaching one – you are selling an idea, not lessons. Used correctly, the extended training period required by the arrival of the Theory Test can become a powerful catalyst for change.

None of this can happen, of course, without the intelligent and committed participation of the ADI. In a very real sense, ADIs will reap what they sow at this, the earliest, and most formative, phase of training. Attitudes to oneself and others, proper road discipline and pride in technique will seep through every moment of an imaginative learning programme. A student who has fully absorbed the message will be a student for life, not just for the weeks or months prior to their driving test.

CHANGING ROLES

With so many advantages to theory tuition, it is both sad and surprising to see how many ADIs fight shy of it. This negative approach springs mainly from the fear of change and a misconception about how difficult theory tuition is. In reality, it isn't very much of a change, and anyone who has survived Parts One, Two and Three of the ADI test is more than equal to the task!

To deliver effective theory training, the ADI must be prepared to undergo a complete and radical transformation that can be summed up as follows: 'You are about to cease functioning as an instructor. You are about to become a teacher.'

2
APPROACHES TO TEACHING

TEACHER VS INSTRUCTOR

If you were to look up the definitions of the terms 'instructor' and 'teacher' in the average dictionary, you would discover that, to all intents and purposes, they are practically the same. If you were to put the same question to the average man or woman, however, you would get two very different answers. The words may seem identical, but each has a distinct emotional 'feel' to it.

Words carry much more than just descriptions. Like a set of Russian dolls, each of which contains a smaller and smaller doll inside, words have hidden depths that shape our attitudes and responses. Consider, for example, how, even out of context and on their own, terms like 'molest', 'pervert', 'taxman' or 'examiner' chill the blood.

The words 'teacher' and 'instructor' come complete with their own cultural baggage as the table overleaf shows. For educational, economic and efficiency reasons, you need to make the transition from instructor to teacher. This change has to take place in your own mind before it can change in those of your students.

Table 2.1 *Teacher vs instructor*

A teacher is ...	An instructor is ...
Someone who teaches valuable lessons for life.	Someone who teaches a knack or trick.
Someone worthy of respect and obedience.	Someone I pay.
Someone who has studied long and hard to perfect difficult skills.	Someone, like me, who can do what I can do but just a bit better.
Someone whose influence can last forever.	Someone I can forget as soon as I have what I want.
Someone who is professional. Someone special.	Someone amateurish. ?

STUDENT EXPECTATIONS

A student is always going to have clear ideas as to what a teacher should look like and how he or she should behave. Despite the fact that teachers in some creative subjects are allowably flamboyant in the public mind, student attitudes are essentially conservative. The student expects the teacher to be an authoritative figure with all that this implies. Any ADI embarking upon theory training work needs to understand this fully for both educational and financial reasons.

The first point to address is whether or not you *look* like a teacher. Too casual a dress style, wild hair-styles and nose studs will focus pupil attention on you rather than on what you are providing and will rob you of credibility. You need to project a solid, professional image that makes the student feel that his or her investment in time and money is worthwhile. A smart jacket or suit announces your intention and transmits subliminal messages, as does the uniform of a policeman, nurse or vicar. An appropriate form of dress can affect the way we respond to people, so take advantage of this basic rule of human behaviour.

A second expectation that students have (even when they do not demonstrate it themselves!) is punctuality. This should really be a non-issue, as the demands of checking premises, equipment, etc should ensure early, not late, arrival. It is a sad fact, however, that many ADIs display poor time-keeping habits, which can have dire consequences. If you are casual in your attitude towards arrival, your students' behaviour will reflect this. They will arrive late, resulting in repetitions or irritation for the other members of the class and possibly a late finish. If you do this often enough, the serious, conscientious students may take their business elsewhere.

Proper time-keeping also carries with it a social message that has a bearing upon the life-skills attitude towards driving. Habits like punctuality go alongside qualities such as consideration and respect for others, and understanding it with regard to theory training may also influence road behaviour at a later date. Set a good example and urge your students to imitate it!

The student expects the teacher to be an authoritative figure in terms of both control and knowledge. Although there is a need to exploit this, you must be careful not to over-play your hand. A stern, overbearing style of teaching will at best alienate your students and at worst lead to open confrontation. An argument is unseemly, will upset the class and, in any case, the student might just be bigger and tougher than you! Eye contact, a subject which will be discussed at length below, is your main control device, not hasty words that cannot easily be retracted. The skills of a leader or a parent, not a commandant, are required here. You cannot demand respect, you must earn it.

19

Authority in the other sense of the word also needs to be tempered with wisdom. Bookish, know-it-all attitudes will prejudice students against higher levels of learning by making them worry that they may become a bore, too ('I don't want to be like *him*!').

You need to function as a teacher rather than as a mere repository of facts, an educator rather than a well-informed anorak. If a student gives a response in good faith that is wrong, let him or her correct it independently rather than just supplying the answer yourself. This will encourage active instead of passive learning. Say, for instance, that during a discussion a student makes a comment that is a clear misinterpretation of traffic rules. You could simply say that he or she is wrong, but would that make for a better or more thoughtful driver? An alternative strategy is to praise the student in a roundabout way and then to get him or her to discover the answer themselves – for example:

ADI:	That's interesting, Kirk, I can see why you said that. There's other ways of looking at it, though. Perhaps we could turn to page 70 and look at the diagram.

The word 'wrong' is conspicuous by its absence here, as it should be. By saying 'That's interesting' you are treating the student with respect; the 'other ways of looking' further distances the student from 'wrong'. Finally, referring back to a text is useful for both the student and other members of the class. Rather than chide or mock, take the student back several mental steps and help him or her to *understand*. Your reward in almost every case will be a flashed smile of relief and a sense of self-satisfaction.

Students also expect teachers to be enthusiastic, even entertaining. (They are a paying audience, after all.) The 'entertainment' that you provide should not be a stream of jokes that might offend in any case, but rather informative material delivered with variety and enthusiasm. Variety is largely a matter of technical competence; enthusiasm is a state of mind that you can practise. Even if you have said what you have to say a thousand times before, you must learn to bring a freshness to it. Unless *you* are interested, nobody else is going to be. Try to treat every talk or demonstration like the first.

Finally, a student expects a teacher to *care*. Each and every student is certain that he or she is the centre of the universe and you have to accept this! Try to get to know each student by name and refer to it every time that you talk to them. Ask your students for opinions, not just answers. On a practical level, if you hear of sickness, injury, etc, send the student a card or at least make a call. Only by such attitudes and actions can you sow the seed for the lifelong bond that you are seeking to develop. You must be what the Japanese call a *sensei*, a teacher whom the student will return to again and again, someone they will always respect.

EYE CONTACT

Good eye contact is an essential part of almost any form of direct training, be it theoretical or practical. The benefits of visual interaction are summed up by the COP formula, which states that proper eye contact allows the trainer to:

- Control.
- Observe.
- Participate.

Control of students in large measure comes down to maintaining good eye contact. This point is so important that it is mentioned throughout this book as something to remember whether you are working directly with a student or through an audio-visual aid such as an overhead projector (OHP).

If you lose regular eye contact with a group, you will also lose control of them unless you are a very gifted orator. As you dwell upon flip-charts or look into space, they will look at each other and ignore your speech. Students may exchange amused glances, or doodle or yawn. Either way, they will change the atmosphere to one of infectious boredom and clock-watching.

You should attempt to engage each student's gaze at least once every minute and more frequently if possible. Try to develop a constantly shifting and interested way of looking at individual members of the group rather than at the group itself. By doing this, you will ensure that many forms of unconsciously disruptive behaviour are stopped before they really start.

Observation is the most basic function of the eyes, but it is astonishing how few trainers remember this in practice. As you let your eyes move from face to face, watch out for signs of boredom, frustration or puzzlement. Note body language and posture at the same time. If you register many such expressions or 'closed' attitudes, stop talking and ask for feedback. Should this be only one individual, however, try to involve him or her by asking for a comment.

Participation is the third key element embodied in the COP principle. Eye contact means involvement and that makes for more effective learning. A talk delivered with good visual cues is far more exciting than a straight lecture and the student will remember the points covered because of this. He or she will also feel important and (literally) looked after.

ASPECTS OF BODY LANGUAGE

As discussed earlier, the most important thing of all in group tuition is student control. If you are weak in this respect, you will be left with a fractious and anarchic mob, and a wish that you had never bothered in the first place as they question everything from your price to your parentage! Eye contact is the most important weapon you have in this struggle for dominance, but the rest of your body also sends out non-verbal messages that you can exploit.

The fact that, as human beings, we have evolved speech tends to blind us to the fact that most animals use other methods of communication. In common with all the rest, however, we transmit information to those around us through gesture, posture and stance. The power of this so-called 'body language' should not be underestimated in dealing with groups. Such unconsciously made signs can betray your innermost feelings, can flatly contradict what you are saying and can influence the way that students respond to you both as a trainer and as a person.

To illustrate this principle through a very simple example, close your eyes for a moment and think about a 'teacher'. It is more than likely that you will have conjured up a picture of someone standing by a board speaking to a group of seated pupils. It is the standing and sitting part of the picture that are the most significant and telling details. The teacher stands up as he or she literally talks down to seated pupils. Everyone else in the room is in a passive, receptive position; only the teacher speaks and everyone else listens. Even when silent, the teacher still dominates by virtue of his or her standing position. The teacher is in control. The situation is even more favourable if the teacher takes to walking around the classroom, peering over students' shoulders, their books, and so on.

You should take advantage of the above principle at all times when teaching, except when you are using an OHP or slide projector, when good technique requires you to be seated. Move in, out and around your students as you speak so that they will have to shift to take in your words. Thus, you will have psychologically 'wrong-footed' them. Additionally, any students who are disposed to gesture to others or to fool about will behave themselves lest you loom up behind them. During most of their formative years, students will have had these behavioural patterns drummed into them by other teaching professionals and it would be a pity not to take advantage of this fact.

Another 'power play' you can use is the chair straddle. Say, for instance, a student wants to get into a vexatious discussion that you would rather avoid because it will impede the rest of the class. You could, of course, remain standing and just slap the student down, but this might not have the desired effect. It might also affect how other students respond to you because you will have behaved in an authoritarian manner without 'winning' the point. Sitting, however, would lower you to the same level as the student and would be tantamount to handing over control. So what should you do?

The alternative is to sit, but to sit in such a way that proclaims that you are still the boss. Take a chair and (unless you are wearing a skirt!) turn it around so that its back faces the audience, and straddle it. Rest your arms on top of the chair and look over the top at the students. Now you are 'king of the castle', speaking from a defended position in which you are harder to 'attack'. You are seated but in a very different fashion from the rest of the group, and this proclaims your leadership.

On those occasions when you do have to sit in a conventional style, be particular how you cross and lock your legs.

The legs can serve as a defensive barrier and if you cross them 'away' from the class, you can make them feel shut out, especially if you have folded your arms.

Standing positions also require some comment. Putting yourself in front of 20 or 30 pairs of eyes can make you feel naked and vulnerable. It is a perfectly natural reaction in such a spot to put up barriers, but you must learn not to in order to be fully effective. Folded arms are out, as are hands clasped in front of the groin. If you must do something with your sweaty, nervous hands, put them *behind* your back in the position favoured by royalty and other VIPs. This, too, is a real 'power' gesture. By leaving yourself unguarded, you are displaying your confidence and freedom from fear of attack. The position will even make you *feel* better; pause for a moment and try out the two different approaches. In the former, your shoulders are pulled in to leave you feeling closed up and weak; in the latter your shoulders and your whole attitude are opened out. Do it now and feel the change it makes in you.

Perhaps the hardest thing to do is to rid yourself of unconscious face-touching gestures. These can range from nose rubs and ear pulls to neck rubs and head scratches. Every one of these gestures carries a meaning, just as much as the words printed on this page. Actions in which you touch or obscure your mouth usually, but not always, go together with telling lies; a neck or ear scratch means that you don't believe a word of it, no matter what you say!

Clothes, too, can get involved in sending out body language signals. A jacket or suit was recommended earlier for class work, but how you wear it says as much as the style of it. Generally speaking, a buttoned-up jacket should only be worn for the first 15 seconds in which you want to stamp your authority. You should quickly unbutton it to show that you are not hiding anything or carrying concealed weapons. (Honestly, clothes do convey such meanings!) Even better, take off your jacket as you get down to serious work. You will very rarely see a top-class trainer talking or demonstrating with a coat on by choice; aside from obvious practical considerations, it indicates a lack of confidence.

Students with tightly crossed arms are angry or scared. You will need more than words to get through this armour, so pause and ask them why they are upset. They will instinctively open up and you can take control once more.

All of the above gestures, and more, can be used in a one-to-one situation just as well. The trick is to recognise these elements in yourself and others, then to apply the positive gestures in a manner that allows you to dictate what is happening. This will take study and practice, but after a while you will begin to use it unconsciously in both teaching and social contexts. The sense of power that this engenders will soak all the way through your group and individual tuition.

The teacher is not the only person who is flashing non-verbal signals left, right and centre, of course. As you hold forth, your students will also strike varying poses and attitudes which you should learn to 'read'. The body language your students demonstrate will teach you more about your effectiveness as a trainer than what is said to you.

People who are sat listening to a talk invariably give the game away by how they react physically. Eye rubbing, neck scratching and ear pulling have already been mentioned, and you should be on the look-out for them. If you see these signs persistently, ask the student to say what he or she is thinking. Watch out too for head-propping gestures which usually indicate boredom.

Foot- and finger-tapping also need to be noticed and dealt with. These are not boredom responses as much as mounting frustration; the tapper is angry and wants to say something but is unable to. A student who taps their feet or drums their fingers will disrupt the rest of the class if they are ignored and will leave the rest of the group feeling irritable. If you catch someone doing this, ask them a question; if they do it again, ask them another one. The idea will sink in eventually and, wonder of wonders, they will be still.

SPEAKING OUT

If you have never spoken to groups before, then expect to find it harrowing. The good news, however, is that your competency in this area can be developed to the point where people consider you a natural orator, someone born with the 'gift of the gab'. The only difference between a poor public speaker and a good one is proper training.

In the sections that follow, a few of the more obvious pitfalls are touched upon. Before that, however, it is worth mentioning a few of the physical and mental points that relate to group talks.

The first thing to remember is that you must be audible. You must learn to speak out and 'up'. Breath control is vital; your words need to be like boats that sail out on a strong tide. You must learn to speak from your stomach rather than from your throat. This is what is called 'projection'. If you master this technique, then your whisper will still be heard at the back of a large hall (provided it is a stage whisper, of course).

The best thing you can do, as will be said repeatedly, is to consult an actor or a speech tutor. Failing that, begin by reading aloud in the largest space that you can find. If you are using a good technique, your throat will feel fine; if you are not, then it will hurt. From this stage, you can move to the great outdoors. Find a lonely hillside and talk at the wind for some time (do check that you are alone, though). Return home and be prepared to be amazed at how much you have improved.

Posture is also important. If you stand stiffly or cramped up, it will stop you breathing in the way that you need to for projecting your voice. Stand upright; clutch the sides of a table to stop yourself shaking if you have to, but stand upright!

On the mental plane, try to imagine that you are talking to one person not dozens, and furthermore to one person whom you know very well. Under normal circumstances, you would not find saying what you have to say to one person intimidating, so try to keep this attitude.

The other hurdle to overcome is preparation. Preparation is one of the secrets of effective teaching. If you know your subject, you can cope!

PACE

If you talk too fast without pausing for breath, then your students will miss most of what you are saying and misunderstand what little they do catch. On the other hand, if you drone on and on, they are not likely to benefit either because they will have fallen asleep! Pace – the speed at which you speak and the way you vary it – is a key element in speaking to a group and one which you should exploit to the full.

The main thing to be said about the rate at which you speak is to vary it, depending on the context of what you are saying. What is too fast and too slow changes according to need and there is no set number of words per minute that you should aim at. A joke, for instance, requires quick-fire delivery, whereas a solemn warning or a recommendation may have to be taken a word at a time. The key is variation according to your own inner clock. Generally speaking, you should talk speedily and briefly when you want to attract attention or to excite, and use a more deliberate pace when you want students to think and relax. Never confuse speed, however, with gabbling. Each and every word you use must be kept 'clean' and distinguishable from the next.

A good exercise that will assist you in obtaining both good 'acceleration' and clear delivery is to read aloud. Start with a novel that you are familiar with. Stand up and read aloud to an invisible audience in a strong, confident voice. The quotation marks used for indicating dialogue are very helpful in this situation; as a rule, when you see them you know that you should talk more urgently or even let your voice linger in a question.

Next, try to tackle a textbook (the duller the better for this purpose). Play a game with yourself in which you try to make the most boring of sentences sound exciting! Try to talk faster and faster. Then, suddenly revert to a more measured, deliberate pace. It doesn't matter if you do not understand a word of what you are saying. Indeed, if you succeed in getting the tempo right, an audience composed entirely of non-English speakers will be intrigued if you read a telephone directory out to them. Variations in tempo help to retain interest and that is your aim.

PITCH

This is closely related to pace. Uniformity of delivery can make for boredom just as much as an unvarying speed. 'Pitch' is all about the rise and fall, the key and tone, of your voice. If you listen to a conversation you will notice that the words used slide up and down the scale to register emotion. Try to say 'What?' in as many different ways as you can – angrily, flatly, softly. Even if a person only heard you say this one word, they would take their emotional cues from the way that you said it.

Never continue in the same tone for more than a few sentences, especially if you are reading aloud. On the other hand, if you are reading aloud, avoid using silly voices unless you are really good at them. To attempt funny voices unsuccessfully may expose you to ridicule rather than to get your point across.

Once you have found a book with plenty of dialogue, practise reading aloud and tape-record the result. Repeat the exercise again with the same passage until you are satisfied with the result. (Try to listen to audio books as well. Also recommended is the appropriate section in *Practical Teaching Skills For Driving Instructors*).

SESQUIPEDALIANISM

The Romans, not the Greeks, invented the word 'sesquipedalian', which is used to describe words that are a foot-and-a-half long. It was used as a jibe against those writers or speakers who tried to impress by using big words just for the sake of it.

Never use a long word if you can get away with a simpler one. (You can use big words to good effect from time to time, though – for example, when you want to puzzle in order to attract attention.) Go through your scripts and prune them of excessively complicated terms which will hide the point you are trying to make. Avoid jargon or techno-speak, too. Not everyone in your audience will use the same jargon for the same instructions or procedures, and 'in' vocabulary can make those unfamiliar with it feel like outsiders.

Never use a dozen words when one will do. Talking at great length about nothing in particular is a sure sign that you do not know the subject you are dealing with well enough, and an audience will soon spot this waffle and lose interest. Say what you have to say simply and briefly.

ON-GOING SELF-DEVELOPMENT

There are a number of measures you can take to develop your theory tuition skills to yet higher levels. The first and foremost of these is to undertake an appropriate City & Guilds course, which will not only equip you with a sound learning base, but will provide you with a certificate that you can use in marketing yourself as well. Much the same can be said for short classroom skills courses that are run by the Driving Instructors Association (DIA) and other bodies. All of these are more than worth the small amount of time or money that you will be required to put into them.

Another route, and one which is recommended several times in this book, is to seek the services of a drama teacher or drama group. The technique known as 'improvisation', in which you and others act 'in character' as you work through a particular situation, is especially useful. Exercises like this will prepare you fully for role-playing games and will furthermore remove any lingering inhibitions you may have. More than any other sort of training, this will help you to 'think on your feet' and to bring life even to the dullest of sessions.

Finally, you should not ignore the vast amount of literature that is available to help you. Listed in Appendix 3 are a number of titles which, in turn, have their own appendices dealing with every conceivable problem that you are likely to encounter. Set aside one evening a week for self-study time. This need not be a chore – most of the books recommended are highly readable and will make you look at many aspects of driving instruction in a different light. Put on some background music, fix a drink or whatever else it takes to make you relax, and go to work. Self-study time can be very rewarding, but, like everything else in life, you only get out what you put into it.

3
FORM AND STRUCTURE

TRAINING METHODS AND STRUCTURES

There are a number of ways in which you can deliver effective theory tuition, each with its own particular merits and demerits. Although in practice one blurs into the other, for our purposes two main categories can be said to exist, which are:

1. Open/distance learning.
2. Directed training.

Open or *distance learning* is, as its name suggests, conducted away from the classroom. Students who use this approach work from home at their own pace, using videos or notes provided. The actual teaching input is small, and a great deal depends on the individual pupil's self-discipline. The ADI in this context is, in fact, more of a guide than a teacher.

Directed training is the kind that most people are familiar with from both school and work. Active tuition is given in person to the individual or groups, often in the formal setting of a classroom or a centre.

Neither of these options is mutually exclusive; they often overlap, and a good, integrated training programme will use elements of both.

At its most basic, the open learning approach asks little of the ADI; all he or she has to do is recommend a few books and supply the occasional question paper. The paper can be marked at the next meeting or, if an easier life is sought, the student can be supplied with an answer sheet. The most extreme version of this approach is correspondence training, which is useful in rural areas where population densities are low. However, it is difficult to see why a student who is capable of working in such a way would bother with an ADI.

For many students, open learning is all that is required – to get them through their Theory Test, at any rate. However, apart from the fact that such students might decide to teach themselves, cramming for an examination from books alone is not going to lead a student to a life-skills approach to driving.

Directed theory training offers the teacher the chance to influence more people more profoundly. Working with small groups or full classes, the ADI is able to make abstract points hit home with the force of a hammer. Students all too readily forget lines they have learned by rote to get through a multiple-choice examination; they will forget less readily, however, the seeping horror of an accident case study or the passion of a 'drink-drive' role play. Directed theory training enables you to shape pupil attitudes and responses for life.

The ideal compromise is an integrated programme that contains all aspects of training. Like a body-builder who 'hits' a muscle from different angles with a variety of exercises, you can develop theory skills by combining home study with group sessions, driving and other instruction. The result of having theoretical principles constantly in view like this will result in real understanding rather than mere knowledge.

WHERE AND WHEN

Open learning makes few demands on the ADI's resources as student work is carried out in his or her personal space and time. More active theory training, however, requires premises. The size of these is dictated by the number of students you want to work with at any given time.

Midway between the car and an actual training centre is (metaphorically speaking) the ADI's own home. The use of an instructor's domestic premises for theory training is nothing new, of course, and there is a good deal to be said for it. It is, above all else, inexpensive. There are no worries about rent, suitability, bookings, etc, and the setting is very informal, which in itself is a big help when dealing with nervous students. Furthermore, some of the equipment used in training, such as the television and video, will normally be set up and ready for use. Finally, if students don't show up for their lesson, you will not have wasted any time travelling to see them.

Home-based tuition does have its problems, however. For a start, there is a limit to the number of students you can accommodate, with consequences to both your profitability and the length of your working week. The domesticity, too, that is a comfort to some pupils will be a disadvantage to others who will compare you unfavourably with a 'class act'. Most serious of all, though, is the effect that this is going to have on your partner and children. Do you and your partner *really* want an endless procession of people invading your own personal space?

ASSESSMENT

A formal assessment of a new student's capabilities is a good idea in all cases, but it is especially important for those who come to you after having failed the Theory Test several times already. The object of the exercise is more than just finding out what they have done so far and what needs to be revised. Your main purpose is to discover whether or not the student has a genuine learning difficulty that is perhaps hard to openly admit to a stranger – for example, illiteracy or dyslexia. It is a good idea, too, at this stage, to ask about the student's health. Medical conditions such as diabetes or high blood pressure can flare up in stressful situations, so do ask students about their health. (Most importantly, if a student declares such a problem, find out what symptoms they might display and what action you should take.)

Such general information should then be followed by a sample test paper. Try to make this experience as authentically uncomfortable as you can. Time them, observe them, and so on, and see how they react to mild stress. However, do warn them what you are doing and why.

Mark the paper there and then. Not only does this add immediacy, it further allows you to demonstrate your expertise as you deftly tick off the correct answers. The theoretical assessment, like a practical one, is as much a sale as a diagnosis. A student will also be assessing *you* as a potential teacher, who might or might not be worth paying money to.

Double-check the student's reading ability by casually asking him or her to read back a few questions to you. People with low literacy levels are not necessarily stupid and they soon learn how to survive in a world full of strange symbols. Multiple-choice tests are simple ('I can read, I just didn't know the right answer'). It benefits no one, least of all the student, to slip through the net, so do make sure of the student's reading ability. (If you do have a student with a reading difficulty, refer them to a suitable tutor in your area.)

Remember to keep the completed test paper. At a later stage you might want to use it as a motivator if the student feels that he or she is making little progress.

The next step is to take your findings and, together with the student, design an action plan – that is, a straightforward plan of how you intend to get the student through the tests (see page 38). Although this sounds horribly 'paperwork-ish', it is actually quite a simple measure and one that will help both of you in equal, if differing, ways. The action plan offers the student a chance to get involved, to feel that he or she is 'doing' rather than been done to; for yourself, the action plan offers a chance to achieve a definite sale, which is your aim.

An action plan offers a tremendous boost to the sale because it seems to provide the 'extra value' beloved of advertisers. If you look closely, however, you will discover that most of the extra value comes from the student rather than from yourself. This point does not figure in the sale, though, as the potential driver sees the exciting timetable appear on paper. Seeing, as they say, is believing.

The example shown begins life as any empty form. On to this you fill in the activities that will create a course. Make sure that both the Theory and Practical Test dates appear in a different colour. Explain to the student what is required and why, adding items as you talk – for example, Monday, week one, Highway Code video.

As more and more squares are completed, the student really will feel that he or she is getting excellent value for money. The fact that your involvement is minimal in many cases will not detract from the power of this presentation. It

Student Action Plan

Name ..... A. LEARNER

Recommendation .... 1 MONTH INTEGRATED TRAINING COURSE

Theory test date ..... 1st AUGUST   Practical test date ..... 10th SEPT

Work Schedule

	Mon	Tue	Wed	Thu	Fri	Sat	Sun	Notes
Week 1	WATCH HIGHWAY CODE VIDEO	LESSON 2-4		LESSON 2-4	THEORY CLASS 730	REVISION 9-10.		
Week 2	REVISION 7-8	LESSON 2-4	REVISION 6.30-7.0	LESSON 2-4	MOCK TEST THEORY			
Week 3								
Week 4								

also serves to remind the student what his or her part of the deal is, and that any missed sessions are inviting failure.

The assessment can be carried out in the car, in the training centre, in your own home or in the student's home. The last option is extremely useful when working with younger drivers as it allows you to present yourself to the decision-makers – that is, the parents.

OFFERING ALTERNATIVES

Because of the wide variations in students' abilities and requirements, it is unlikely that any one programme will suit all of them. The tuition that will bore one learner may be just right for another, and this can cause real problems. For both educational and business reasons, you need to offer a selection of training options that move at different speeds.

Following assessment (see page 36), you should grade or 'stream' students according to their individual capabilities and problems. This can be done with reference to ability or, alternatively, their age. Older learners might feel uncomfortable among a group of bright youngsters, and the reverse can also be true. (A class composed entirely of young students is not without its problems, however. For reasons of discipline and support, it is advisable to mix in some older, brighter learners.)

It is advisable at this stage to segregate multiple-test failures, especially those who have come to you from another instructor. Not only do they have obvious difficulties, they will carry with them attitudes and responses which might infect other groups. Think how a single drop of ink can discolour an entire bottle of milk and remember to keep such demotivating pupils well quarantined!

The upshot of all this activity is to leave you in a position whereby you can offer the potential driver several 'lanes' that he or she can choose to travel in. The 'fast lane' will contain those who wish to pass very quickly and who are willing to undertake integrated theory/practical training. To these can be added the steady influx of students from elsewhere who have already completed their Theory Test. (Bearing in mind the life-skills approach you are seeking to develop, you should encourage even those who join up exclusively for driving to attend a few group sessions. Role-plays, etc would be especially useful in this context.)

The next lane is reserved for those who want to proceed at a more relaxed rate. For some of these the theory sessions will take on the role of a social occasion, and they may well want to continue this aspect of training even after their examination.

Finally, there is always going to be a 'crawler' lane packed with nervous or challenged students who are intent on 'doing one thing at a time'. These, too, may be with you longer than the average pupil, but for very different reasons.

You must be very careful, of course, how you present these options to a prospective customer. There must be no stigma attached to any of the groups, no hint that some students may not be intelligent. Be sure that your recommendations are positive ones that leave the student feeling as if he or she has had a tailor-made training programme. And remind them, too, that they can switch lanes any time they want.

Before you groan about the amount of 'administration' or reorganisation that this approach involves, think for a moment how it will affect your business. Pupil scarcity should be a thing of the past because you will have many little pools that you can keep dipping into. Or again, you will be like a farmer who sows one sort of crop at the same time as reaping others that have come to maturity. Such a blessing in disguise is not to be sneered at.

4

CENTRE-BASED TRAINING

CENTRE APPRAISAL

If, after due deliberation, you decide in favour of group, centre-based training, the next thing you need to do is to locate premises which are suitable for the job. This may sound easy, but in reality the process of hiring out has all the pitfalls and catches of buying a house. The big issues, such as how much you can afford and the number of students you wish to cater for, should have been decided already and the rest are just 'details'. They are, however, very important details.

Shown overleaf (Table 4.1) is a Centre Appraisal Sheet, a copy of which you should fill out for every promising location that you visit. Do not allow your enthusiasm and need blind you to faults or deficiencies. A poor decision at this stage will cost you both time and money later on, so it is vital that you pay attention to matters that you might consider quite trivial. In the end, it is the silly little things that most often cause the biggest headaches, so be on the look-out. Work on a 'worst case scenario'; if a student vandalises a toilet or breaks things accidentally, who is responsible? What will your own moral and financial obligations be in such an eventuality?

Table 4.1   *Centre appraisal sheet*

Feature	Notes
Location with regard to car tuition	
Image	
Access via public transport	
Car parking	
Male/female toilets	
Cloakroom	
Heating/ventilation	
Lighting	
Tables and chairs	
Fire-doors	
Fire-extinguishers	
First-aid box	
Power points	
Screen/projection surface	
Floor surface	
Floor space	
Tea/coffee facilities	
Contract	
Cost	
Contact	

Unless good fortune has smiled upon you, it is more than likely that you will be hiring premises at the lower end of the market – for example, church or vestry halls, community centres, etc – in which case a thorough investigation is essential. Even if you are lucky enough to be working from ideal premises such as schools or colleges, you should keep the following comments in mind.

Location

First and foremost, you must decide which is the best area to operate from. If your chosen spot is out of town, then it needs to be as close to home and to your practical driving circuit as possible in order to capitalise on advertising and travel.

An alternative option is to look for premises in the town or city centre that are accessible to all your students.

Desirability/image

This decision may well entail a compromise between what you would like and what you can afford. Other than institutes of education, most places will fall short of your dreams, but factors such as location and better profit margins may help you to soldier on.

There is a point, however, beyond which you should not venture. If the premises chosen look shabby or seedy, this in turn will reflect upon your standards. Such a place sends out all the wrong signals.

Access via public transport

Most of your students will not arrive by car, so pay attention to what public transport is available and what times trains and buses run. (It is a good idea, in fact, to have a timetable on your teaching table.)

Lack of public transport can be a decisive factor in getting students to your class, so give the matter some consideration. At the opposite end of the scale, try not to get too close to a busy main road where the thunder of traffic may prove a distraction.

Car parking facilities

On the other hand, some students *will* arrive by car, so see what sort of facilities are available. The last thing you need is an irate neighbour demanding that a car belonging to one of your students must be moved from 'his' part of the road. A private, secure car park is doubly useful in that it also allows for car maintenance lessons.

Cloakroom facilities

At times students will arrive wet and soggy, so somewhere to hang up coats will prove useful. If no separate facility exists, you could consider purchasing a coat rail or something similar. (As a prospective tenant, you can ask for such items and get a positive response, whereas later you will get a frown.) (NB If a proper cloakroom is used, advise students not to leave valuables in their coat pockets.)

Fire-doors

Find out where these are, whether they actually open and that they are not obstructed.

Fire-extinguishers

Note what models are available and ask how they are best used. You should also check on service dates which are generally attached to them.

Public liability certificate

One of these should be displayed on a wall. Ask for a copy and then let your own broker scrutinise it.

Stairs

Downgrade any premises that involve climbing numerous stairs as these will prove difficult for older or disabled students.

Male/female toilets

These really are essential. When viewing premises, check hot-water supplies and what sort of hand-drying facilities are available. Find out, too, who is responsible for cleaning and the provision of items such as toilet rolls.

Heating/ventilation

It is particularly important that the room temperature is at the right level for sedentary class work. Students shivering in their coats or sweltering in the heat do not make the best of learners! Try to time an inspection visit so that you can see any systems in action.

Be sure that you find out whether the cost of extra heating will be added to your bills. This is very important if you will be sharing the facility with other groups.

First-aid box

Ask where this is and see what it contains. Take your own box as well; larger kits seem to cover every eventuality from broken arms to radiation burns, but often do not contain small plasters.

Canteen facilities

A tea-break or 'social' can sometimes be handy, so ask what there is in the way of kettles, cups and saucers, etc.

Power points

Some audio-visual aids require electricity, so make sure that enough power points are available, and that they work!

Screen/projection surface

Does the centre have a screen for use with an OHP or slide projector? If not, is a good clean wall surface available?

Curtains/blackout

You may need darkened conditions for the effective use of video, OHP, etc. Draw the curtains to see how dark the room becomes.

Tables and chairs

Count how many of these are available. If there is an insufficient number, suggest that you might have to find alternative premises and see if more are provided. By the same token, make sure that any tables and chairs are in good condition. At the start of your first lesson is not the time to discover that some of them are wobbly or unsafe.

Floor space

Now and then you may need floor space for games or role-plays. See what sort of area you have when tables and chairs are stacked.

Floor covering

If you intend to do lots of relaxation exercises or games, a carpet is preferable to other floor coverings.

Telephone

A telephone is desirable for emergencies and for student use. Unless this is a pay-phone, however, keep it well under control. Failure to do so may result in an unexpected bill and nasty words from an aggrieved committee.

A constantly ringing telephone, of course, can be a really distracting influence. Note where it is situated in relation to your prospective teaching room.

Lighting

Good lighting is essential. Try to visit the places on offer by night to get an idea of what conditions will be like then or on dark winter afternoons.

Contract

Most rooms that are available for hire usually offer a contract. You should read through this several times and highlight any particular concerns or clauses you do not understand. As mentioned above, seek to clarify the smallest of details with regard to wear and tear, use, etc.

HEALTH AND SAFETY ISSUES

Taking charge of a group of students means that if someone gets stung by a wasp, feels sick or collapses, you will be responsible for that person. You might just be lucky and have a qualified medical practitioner on hand, but then again you might not. That could mean the difference between life and death for somebody who has put him- or herself in your trust.

The most obvious and sensible precaution you can take against such eventualities is to get yourself trained to deliver first aid. You might feel that you do not have time for this peripheral skill when you have so much else to learn. Make the time. A short course, as well as safeguarding your students and passengers, also offers the following tangible benefits:

1. Increased self-confidence. The extra knowledge that you gain will reinforce your own image as an educator.
2. Documentation that will appear in your press hand-outs or training premises. This could be a significant factor when selling yourself to companies or colleges.
3. New pupils. You will tell other course members what you do, won't you?
4. Further instruction for your own pupils. After developing first-aid skills, it would be a pity not to pass some of them on. Show your students some basic first-aid techniques, such as the recovery position, in training sessions about road accidents.

The benefits of first-aid experience outweigh many times the small investment in time and money that is required. A course is strongly advised.

PREVENTION IS BETTER THAN CURE

The vast majority of accidents, whether on the road, in the home or in the workplace are easily avoidable. To avoid the need for saying 'I should have seen it earlier', draw up a checklist of crucial points that you can work through prior to each training session. Do not cheat on this list or skip through it on the assumption that everything will be the same as it was last week. Try to include the following in your checklist:

- Are the fire-doors open and unobstructed?
- Are the fire-extinguishers in place and in good order?

- Are the plugs and wires of any electrical audio-visual aids in good condition?
- Are you aware of the location of the mains switch and can you get to it quickly?
- Are the male/female toilets in good condition and fully supplied with soap, towels, etc?
- Are heating and lighting systems working properly? Are there any hot surfaces that need to be covered or avoided?
- Are the floors slippery or dangerous with mat edges or other items that could be tripped over?
- Are desks and chairs stable and safe to use?
- Are there any trailing wires from the OHP or TV which might trip up students?
- Is there any rubbish around which might present a fire hazard?

Remember, health and safety matters apply to yourself as well. You may be moving heavy pieces of equipment like televisions, so observe good practice in this area. Do *not* bend over to pick up boxes of books, projectors, etc in a hurry. Bend your knees instead and stand up slowly with the object in your grasp.

A final aspect of this topic which, sadly, must be touched upon, is personal safety. We live in violent times and wherever there is more than one human being, there is potentially a problem. It is a nettle you need to grasp for your own sake and that of your students.

If your training area is off-the-beaten-track or has a dark car-parking space, be very careful as you arrive. Your movements are of necessity well known and regular, and the fact that you are carrying expensive electrical items such as televisions or projectors may not have gone unnoticed. It will also be common knowledge that you charge money for your services and may have a considerable amount of cash with you.

Should you arrive early and unaccompanied, take a precautionary drive around the premises. If you are in any doubt about shadowy presences or unidentified bystanders, stay in your car or drive off. The watchword is caution. Muggings, like road accidents, always seem to happen to someone else. When you do park, leave your car near an illuminated space or occupied homes.

During the class itself, keep an eye open for possible flashpoints. Try to defuse nasty situations by use of body-language skills and soft words. If a student rounds on you personally, do not argue directly. Keep your distance both literally and metaphorically, and allow the bully to let off steam. Nine times out of ten, irate students will turn bright red in the silence that follows their outburst and then storm out, much to the relief of yourself and the other members of the group.

Occasionally, however, a really confused student may want to inflict actual bodily harm. You have only three possible responses in this situation. The first is to run away, a course which is recommended whenever it is available. Do not rely on other people to spring to your defence; they will be as paralysed as you are for a few seconds, and a few seconds is all it takes to get badly hurt. It is best to get out of harm's way.

Your second option is to stand there and take it. In this case, cover your head and vital areas and make as much noise as possible. If you get knocked to the floor, curl up and pretend to be in more distress than you are. This in itself will satisfy some aggressors.

The third option is to stand your ground and/or to fight back. The question of whether it is better to resist or yield to an attack is hotly debated by all experts in this area, and there seems to be no definitive answer. It can be and is argued that any form of resistance will only escalate levels of violence, and that any form of counter-offensive may well be illegal in its own right. On the other hand, there is a more pragmatic attitude which can be summed up by the popular American dictum 'Better be judged by twelve than carried by six'. The worried ADI is best advised to consider basic self-defence training; those who are not so worried should at least attempt to frame their mental and physical responses to such an occurrence. Situations like this are very rare, but there is no point pretending that they do not happen – ask any teacher.

There is, in actual fact, more likelihood of violent behaviour being directed against other students than against yourself. If you are dealing with younger groups, both male and female, then class interaction can take some very strange turns. This may range from a complaint such as 'He (or she) was looking at me funny' to a statement such as 'She was asking for it'. Racial abuse and sexual harassment are facts of life, and you may find these, too, creeping in insidiously.

Be alert to friction among pupils and intervene verbally to allow the students involved to retreat without losing face. At the end of the session, watch over the victims of abuse or threats as they leave and ensure that they get home safely.

Finally, on this sorry subject, be careful as you leave the centre. In most cases you will be carrying more money out than you went in with, and this can make you a tempting target. Consider the possibility of carrying a personal alarm, but, more importantly, keep your eyes and ears open.

5

THE RECRUITMENT AND RETENTION OF THEORY STUDENTS

SELLING POINTS

In the companion volume to this title, *The Driving Instructor's Guide to Effective Selling Skills*, one simple truth is hammered home repeatedly: before you can teach, you must first sell. No matter how great your technical proficiency, no matter how good your resources, unless you can get students to come back on a regular fee-paying basis, your efforts are in vain. This fact applies even more to theory training, which in itself lacks the seductive, hands-on appeal of practical work.

To obtain the quantity and quality of students that you need, a clear marketing strategy is required. Take a blank sheet of paper, then ask yourself the following questions:

- How many students do I want?
- What kind of students are they?
- What do I intend to offer them?
- What makes me different, unusual?
- What do I have that the competition lacks?

Each of these points merits some serious thought. How many

new potential students you need to see per week, per month, per year depends to a large extent on the system that you choose to operate. A small, home-based set-up, for example, will not require the same kind of advertising push that a centre-based approach does.

The kind of student that you get is partly a matter of choice, partly a matter of circumstance. You can advertise specifically for a certain type of student or just take whoever responds to a more general message. Be warned, however, that most of the students who actively seek tuition for what is, after all, a fairly simple examination, are going to have declared or undeclared learning problems.

The above point has implications for what you intend to offer. Under this heading, too, come any extras that you are going to provide – for example, free lessons on failure, learning aids, etc.

Defining what you intend to provide will also reveal, in many cases, what is different about your service and why a student should choose you. It is essential that you are able to describe this and the other points to yourself. Only when that process is complete can you begin to sell what you have to others.

EFFECTIVE ADVERTISING

It goes without saying, of course, that the words 'theory training' should henceforth appear in any advertising that you engage in. This on its own, though, is unlikely to get students lining up at the door. Many other people are determined to pick the same lucrative cherry, and to beat them to it, your advertising will need to be very effective.

The rule-of-thumb that you need to apply to advertising is that the less it actually says, the better it works. Do not give away too much information or you will be giving away customers. You need to keep things under control for economic reasons, but, more importantly, you need to tantalise the prospective customer. The purpose of most advertising is to create the desire to make a phone call. If you say everything that needs saying in print, then you rob yourself of the opportunity to do some active selling.

Compress the things that make you distinctive into a single sentence. At this stage, prune the sentence still further by removing any stray words. Remember always, therefore, that the purpose of an advertisement in this context is to create a need for further information, not to satisfy it.

Use modern terms wherever you can. The term 'theory lessons', for instance, is rather old-fashioned. The prospective student might say to him- or herself, 'I had lessons and they didn't work.' If, however, instead of offering lessons you offer 'learning modules', you might just excite someone's curiosity to the point where he or she simply has to pick up the telephone and enquire.

You will find more on how to design advertisements and how to convert the calls that follow into bookings in *The Driving Instructor's Guide to Effective Selling Skills*.

ACTIVE PROSPECTING

There are methods other than advertising to obtain new students. All advertising is hit-and-miss and works like a scatter-gun. At the end of the day, however, its biggest problem is that it is passive – that is, it depends on someone doing something about it. A different technique called 'active prospecting' is ideally suited to theory marketing and will put you in control of the process.

SEMINAR SELLING

Seminars are used to sell a great many products – financial services, holidays, timeshares and ADI training, to name but a few. They are, in addition, perfectly suited to the selling of centre-based theory tuition, and the ADI who learns to master this particular technique can expect to reap handsome rewards.

The essence of a seminar is this: 30 or 40 potential customers, or 'prospects', are invited to a brief show concerning a service or product. This leads to a questions-and-answers session and an invitation to purchase whatever is offered.

There is, of course, a great deal more to seminar selling than the above paragraph, but the ADI should not feel unduly nervous about exploring the concept. The basic skills required are no different from those employed in group theory training. Only the aim of the seminar, the goal, is different: business seminars are about selling, not telling.

A theory seminar aimed at the 'general' public needs little in the way of specialised advertising. Indeed, the less said the better. No more than is absolutely necessary should be divulged at this stage – for example, you could say 'Free Theory Test seminar: call 1234567'. Your aim is to tantalise and get 'bums on seats' in sales parlance.

It is also possible to look for specific client groups if you feel that you have a service to offer or if there is a niche in your local market. You might advertise, for instance, for multiple-test failures, older learners, the under-17s, etc. A campaign can be designed around this – for instance, you could do a mail-shot targeting new drivers by studying the electoral rolls in your local library. As with all forms of advertising, however, the cost-benefits aspect of the campaign needs to be kept under close review. In general, the simpler and cheaper the methods you employ, the greater will be your profits. Start with the very simple measure of handing out invitations to existing students for them to give to their friends.

The actual content of the seminar must be sufficient to occupy 30 or 40 minutes at the most. Visual aids should figure prominently, the best two for the job being the slide projector and the overhead projector. The most important item is the script, which you must write and rewrite until it is as near-perfect as possible. Use the same principles outlined elsewhere in this book and when it is finished, stage a rehearsal for a friendly, but honest audience.

The slides or acetates you employ are also of crucial importance. Try to get a mixture of ones that are very serious, such as road accidents, and ones that are very funny, such as cartoons. Unless you are artistically gifted, you may need some help with these, but spend time and money to get them right. Bear in mind that just one effective seminar could set you up with enough students to last you two or three months.

On the actual day or evening of the seminar, a partner or friend who is willing to act as a host or hostess can prove invaluable. Not only will their presence boost your confidence, it will also enhance your successful image as the audience concludes that you can afford paid staff. The main function of your help, however, is to gather the names and addresses of those present, which can be done with a questionnaire. If anyone asks why you are collecting names, tell them quite honestly that it is for future mail-shots about driving-related matters.

Seminars are also very portable. You can take the show 'out on the road' to clubs, schools, colleges and companies, where you can also trawl for students requiring practical lessons. This is excellent winter work and eliminates the need for costly advertising.

OPEN-HOUSE TRAINING

Although this form of training is less cost-effective than a formal seminar, it does have its place. Essentially, what you are doing is a mini-seminar for six to eight students at the most, presented in the comfort of one of their homes. (Ideally, it should be in the home of a pupil who has completed a full training cycle, both theory and practical, with you.)

This approach works very well with ethnic minority groups where cultural restrictions may impede movement. The open house then develops into open-house training conducted according to whatever social values apply. It can also be appropriate for the under-17s where watchful parents can see what their children are doing.

Open-house sessions obviously will not yield the same sort of new pupils as a seminar proper. On the other hand, it is less demanding and will localise your work.

OPEN DAYS/EVENINGS

An open day or evening at your centre is a less structured, but still very effective, method of presenting your services to the public. Your centre is open between certain hours as a kind of drop-in place where you may be consulted about all manner of driving problems. (The exact time and day obviously depend upon centre availability and its location/ease of access.)

The advertising campaign for your event should begin at least one month in advance of the chosen date. Window cards or A4-sized posters are cheap, cheerful and easy to make. It is also possible that local papers or magazines would be interested enough to run a short paragraph if you stress the safety aspects of your session. At this stage, do not forget to enlist your students' help; they may have notice-boards at work, and friends or family who might be of use.

The training room should be set out much as usual, but without the tables that you would normally put out for students. Use these, instead, for items of interest that visitors can wander around in their own time. One table should have samples of test papers that people can attempt. Another should display the latest publications you have for sale or that you utilise in the course-work. If possible, set aside a corner for the video with a few chairs and play a tape at low volume. Any other aids that you have, from slide projector to flip-chart, should also be pressed into service. These need to operate without over-much involvement on your part, however. You must be free to chat, smile and, above all, sell.

Tea, coffee and soft drinks are essential. Disposable plastic cups are preferable for reasons of time and hygiene. A partner, friend or student would be most useful to help serve the drinks.

If your centre is difficult to find, put a small map on any publicity. Likewise, try to have a board or sign positioned outside for the last few uncertain steps.

Station yourself at a table near the door and make sure you

have pen, paper and business cards available. As visitors arrive, remember the previous comments about body language and, above all, smile. Your ADI badge pinned on your jacket is a real bonus; it will both identify you and give you status.

The event you are holding aims to present you as someone who can help with almost any sort of driving problem, and you should bear this in mind.

During the day, you are going to be asked numerous questions, so do read up all information and have a full set of textbooks at hand for the really tricky questions. Also, have a pile of driving licence and test applications available. (Almost certainly someone will quiz you about LGV/PCV legislation; rather than look blank, revise the subject and make contact with a school that provides tuition in these vehicles. If you strike a commission deal with them, you could well cover your costs for the day.)

There are various other people with an interest in your potential clients to whom it might be worth offering a table – for example, your insurance broker, a car dealer or an alarm specialist. As well as adding a little colour, they may well contribute to advertising or refreshment expenses; they will certainly be a set of eyes when you need to leave the room or sort something out. It does no harm, in any case, to do a bit of networking. If they put on shows of their own, you might get an invitation in return.

Open days can be very profitable if you put sufficient thought into them. Like most things, they are all about preparation and imagination. The following are a few of the services you might want to sell at such an event:

- Theory training for the under-17s.
- Theory training for older learners.
- Car training for the practical driving test.
- Problem-solving modules for multiple-test failures.

- Refresher courses.
- Theory tests for parents.
- Defensive or Advanced driving.

- LGV/PCV commissions.
- Car insurance.
- Car alarms, security devices.
- Car accessories.
- Breakdown insurance/warranties.
- Books.
- Videos.
- Highway Codes.
- ADI training.

PAYMENT IN ADVANCE

You should tell students that paying in advance for theory training is good for them, the reason being that the act of paying in advance is symbolic as well as actual. It represents commitment and the desire to succeed, no matter what difficulties lie ahead.

Practically, of course, you need to collect fees up-front to protect and stabilise your own cash flow. Your overheads are not likely to go down or disappear, so every unoccupied place you have in your theory-training class is costing you money, just as a cancelled lesson does. The failure to control this aspect of business is one of the chief reasons for the roller-coaster performance of so many ADIs.

There is no point, however, telling students that you want cash in advance to protect your own livelihood, as they will not see this as a valid reason to pay you. An approach like this in truth would cause suspicion and resistance. Students are the centre of the universe, not you. In order to get students' co-operation, therefore, you must sell them the benefits of this course of action.

First, give the reasons mentioned above – they are very real ones and have a bearing on student behaviour, even if only to the extent that people do not like to miss what they have paid for.

You will probably need to offer more tangible benefits, however. One option, if you operate group training, is to offer those who pay in advance free attendance on test failure at further sessions. As this is only likely to involve a small percentage of students and represents no extra cost to yourself, this is a safe route to go down.

An alternative is to use a modification of the 'retainer' concept. In this method, students pay a retainer equivalent to the cost of one or two lessons. If they complete the training programme without missing a session, they get the money back as a 'reward'. (For a full discussion of this method and how to sell it, see *The Driving Instructor's Guide to Effective Selling Skills*.

RECLAIMING LOST STUDENTS

Not every student will complete the course. Some will run out of money, some will be poached, some will disappear through circumstances beyond their control. Some, frankly, will get bored with you. If your business machine is running correctly, this is not going to be too much of a problem. However, for both the students' sakes and your own quality control, you need to understand why they left and make an effort to reclaim them. That process begins with effective record-keeping.

For every student who enrols with you on theory training, make a record card or computer entry. This obviously needs to contain working details such as name and number, but what you really need are the observations that you made during their assessment. (You can, of course, use your fact-find instead of a separate item; the aim is to produce effective paperwork, not reams of it.) What you are looking for in this exercise are any particular worries, learning difficulties or aspirations the students may have had. These will provide you with clues as to what has possibly gone wrong and how to approach the situation.

When a student fails to continue the course, put your records to good use. Make a courtesy telephone call, stressing the word 'courtesy' the moment the phone is answered so that the student does not feel that he or she is being checked up on or pressurised. Students, after all, are paying customers and should not be dealt with like schoolchildren playing truant. (If the phone is answered by someone other than your student, apologise and ring back later.)

After a few seconds of breaking the ice, begin by saying that 'the class has missed you'. An expression like this is much more effective and flattering than putting your own opinion forward and appeals to any social bonds that the student may have made with others. Kindling a positive memory at this stage will assist you greatly if later you have to resell the benefits of theory training.

Next, say that you are a little concerned about the effect that missed training is going to have on their examination performance. Pause for a second and, in a somewhat subdued tone, say that you are also worried in case anything you have said or done has given offence. Usually this will be met by a nervous laugh and words to the effect that you are just wonderful. (On the other hand, if you really have upset the student you will soon know about it!)

Should the student tell you that their absence has been due to sickness, work, etc and that they will resume training the next week, *carry on talking for a while*. If you hang up the moment you have established whether or not they have an excuse, you really will be perceived as a truant officer. The word used was courtesy, so show it!

The way is now clear for a serious discussion about why a student has gone missing. It is vitally important at this stage that you allow the student to voice his or her worries and attitudes in full. Do not contradict or interrupt them, no matter how unfair and distorted their views are. Hear them out and make reassuring comments like 'I see' or 'Do you mind if I write that down?'. To win the war you may have to let them win the battle. Let the student release any frustration or anger, and then come back to the fact that there is still a need to pass the Theory Test, and that you can help with their training.

If, after all this, the student still refuses further training, do not hang up in a huff or on a sore note. Ask if you can ring back in a few weeks after they have passed the Theory Test to keep your records straight. On this next call, you have two selling opportunities. If they have failed, then they may well reconsider your training; if they have passed, invite them out on a practical lesson. If the student tells you that they have found another instructor, this is not necessarily the end of the matter. There is, in fact, a better than 50:50 chance that the student will discover that their preferred choice is actually not as good or as nice as you. Unless you make a follow-up call, you will never get the chance to bring them back into the fold.

6
USING AUDIO-VISUAL AIDS

OVERVIEW

The rapid advance of science has given the modern class-room the feel of a laboratory. No lesson is complete, it seems, without the use of the video, the overhead projector or some other hi-tech appliance.

Make no mistake about it, the many kinds of audio-visual aids on the market can really help the educational process along. They offer variety, stimulation, colour and a host of other important qualities. There is a fundamental principle to keep in mind when using them, however, and that is: *training aids are training aids and not an end in themselves*. The showing of pretty pictures will not salvage a droning, monotonous presentation, nor will the playing of a video cover up the lack of people skills. Lacking the proper human content and control, the impressive pieces of equipment become nothing more than a set of expensive toys. Audio-visual aids will help you to sharpen your teaching skills, but they can never serve as a substitute.

The three classes of equipment that are likely to be of use to the ADI are as follows:

1. The OHP (overhead projector).

2. The video cassette player/television/camera.
3. The slide projector.

Although each of the above items has its own particular applications and requirements, there are a number of rules which apply to all of them.

SEE, HEAR

The first rule to remember when you are using audio-visual equipment – and one which amazingly enough is forgotten by many trainers – is that each student needs to be able to see what is going on. An OHP image that requires the student to adopt an awkward position to see it because it is poorly situated, or a television screen that is lost in the afternoon sun, is worse than useless.

Whatever sort of audio-visual aid you intend to use, ensure that everyone can see it without discomfort. If facilities permit, experiment with different seating plans until you find the one that you and your audience are most comfortable with (see Figure 6.1).

Make sure that the curtains are drawn to keep out sunlight or distracting movements from outside. Eliminate any other sources of light, such as those that show beneath doors, that might be distracting. You and your projected image must remain central to the student.

By the same token, be certain that your students can hear what you or the machine are saying. There is a tendency for people to drop their voices when they are in a darkened room. Practise your routine fully with just the glow of the OHP, or whatever light is available, if you are working in the dark. Set any volume control so that it informs students in the back row

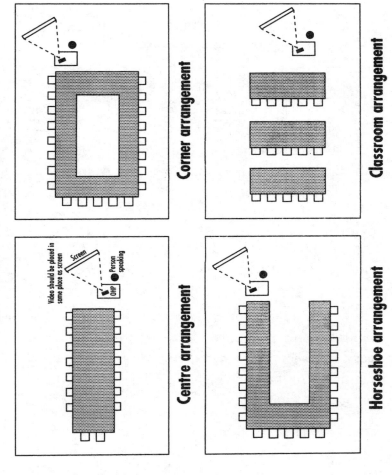

Figure 6.1

71

without deafening those in the front. Experiment and allow for different rooms.

TALK TO THE AUDIENCE

The second rule to remember is that you must talk to your audience and not the machine you are using. Confronted by 20 or 30 expectant faces, it is a perfectly natural reaction to duck for cover, which, in this case, is the television screen or projection. When you talk to the wall, for example, it feels safe, comfortable and harmless.

Although this behaviour is an understandable and normal response to stress, it is one that you cannot afford to let happen. Within seconds of your addressing the screen or projection, you have lost control. Once eye contact is broken, attention wanders and students lose interest. They will start to think about going home, going out or the person next to them, and what you are offering is going to come a very poor second.

When using visual aids, you must learn to keep your back towards them. You must resist, too, the temptation to check every few seconds that the picture is still there. Unless the machine is broken, the picture will not vanish. Maintain eye contact and control!

PLAN, PLAN, PLAN!

The third principle to remember when using visual aids is that of planning and practice. As mentioned earlier, no machine is of itself going to make you a brilliant teacher.

Every word, gesture or joke you use in an audio-visual presentation needs to be scripted and practised in advance.

You also need to plan for the unexpected. If a bulb goes, a fuse blows or a tape jams, what are you going to do about it? So plan ahead for such eventualities.

USING THE OVERHEAD PROJECTOR

The overhead projector is, perhaps, the most useful of all the electrically powered audio-visual aids. Robust, flexible and easy to operate, the OHP is a highly effective tool for presenting information to groups both large and small. The ADI who wants to succeed in classroom-style training should buy one at once and then *learn how to use it*. Unless this last warning is heeded, then the would-be trainer may as well save the expense and continue to use flip-charts or whiteboards.

Overhead projectors have changed little over the years, reflecting the quality of their original design. The newer models are much slimmer, of course, and have a few extras, but their basic concept remains unchanged. An illuminated screen or 'platen' shines through transparent sheets, the image being picked up by a lens and then projected on to a screen. Focusing is achieved by turning a wheel to move the projection head up or down (Figure 6.2). Some models have an internal fan to help the machine to cool down. The more recent versions often have a back-up light which can be switched on in the event of main bulb failure. As far as technical information goes, that is really all you need to know.

The Overhead Projector

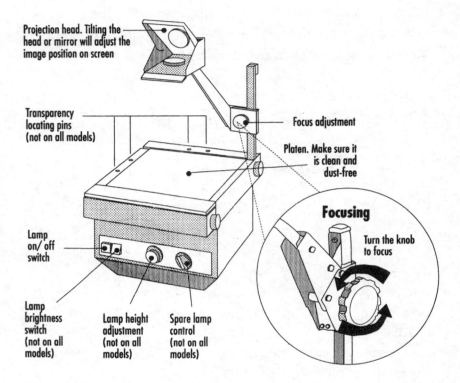

Projection head. Tilting the head or mirror will adjust the image position on screen

Transparency locating pins (not on all models)

Focus adjustment

Platen. Make sure it is clean and dust-free

Lamp on/off switch

Lamp brightness switch (not on all models)

Lamp height adjustment (not on all models)

Spare lamp control (not on all models)

Focusing

Turn the knob to focus

Figure 6.2

LIGHT FITTINGS

The only other part of an OHP that is worth mentioning is the acetate sheet or transparency projected by it. These can be broadly divided into two families – pre-prepared transparencies and 'instant' transparencies that you create as you talk.

Pre-prepared transparencies that deal with driving-related matters are available from most specialist ADI shops. If these fail to excite you, then you can always make your own; unless you are artistically gifted, however, it is probably wiser to have your design executed by a printer or high-street print shop. The extra cost that this entails is more than offset by the difference in the finish. (If you wish to create your own transparencies refer to *Instructional Techniques and Practice for Driving Instructors*.)

Whichever method you use to create your transparencies, the final step is to put them into cardboard mountings. These will help to extend their working life, but of equal importance is the fact that you can then number them and add on key words or points.

The other sort of 'transparency' you can employ is nothing more complicated than a clean acetate sheet on which you write or draw as you speak. This rough-and-ready approach has the charm of spontaneity and also makes students wait for the next line to appear, which helps to keep them awake.

Transparencies of this sort are made with special felt-tipped markers (for thick lines) or fibre-tipped OHP pens (for thin lines and details). You can use either spirit-based or water-soluble markers. The former are excellent for making pre-prepared sheets that you can use time and time again, but are less useful for one-offs as a solvent is required to remove the information from the sheets. Use water-soluble pens instead, which will both save you money and allow for corrections. All you need to do in this case is to wipe the transparency with a damp cloth. Bear in mind, however, that water-soluble pens can also smudge. If your hands are sweaty with nerves, dry them with a cloth before you start to work to avoid smudging your writing.

Have a variety of bold colours available to emphasise different points. Steer clear of yellow, though; it fades into the background whiteness too easily for comfortable reading. Any phrases or pictures that you use should be simple and uncluttered. For maximum effect, use the minimum amount of information per sheet.

STORYTIME

The OHP is described as an *audio*-visual aid, which means that the spoken word is just as important in its correct use as any image you care to put on the screen. Neither 'instant' nor pre-prepared software can get your points across effectively without the aid of a good, tight script. You must ensure that every picture does indeed tell a story by supplying one yourself.

Begin by deciding what your presentation is actually about – for example, road safety, signs, etc. Avoid cramming in too much information or getting caught up in side issues. Keep your presentation simple and straightforward, remembering that these days people's attention span is largely measured by the length of television programmes. If you continue for too long without changing pace or medium, you will lose your audience rather than educate them. If your chosen topic is so big that you cannot cover it in under ten minutes, then make two presentations on separate occasions instead.

Packs bought from specialist shops often have teaching notes included in them. If these are not provided, or if you are creating a presentation from scratch, then you must make your own. Start by spreading out your transparencies on the floor or on a long table in their correct running order. (It is as well to have a title sheet which will allow a few seconds for the audience to settle down and focus.)

Under each transparency place two sheets of blank paper. Now write down bullet-point comments about each acetate in turn. Include in these vital information, key words, mnemonics, and so on. Double-check with textbooks that you have not missed out anything of importance. (The actual bullet points should be written on the acetate mountings in clear lines that can be read in dim conditions.)

The next step is to refine these jottings into four or five sentences. Have a dictionary at your side or, better still, a thesaurus, to avoid boring repetitions. Try to use the same words only once or twice unless you are doing this intentionally for effect. Remember, too, that a question is more effective than a statement to attract people's attention.

By this time, you will have created pearls of wisdom and wit that you can now thread together. The 'thread' that you have created will consist of linking sentences, questions and jokes. Be sparing with the latter – too many jokes will cause your students to think of you as a comedian rather than as an educator. Refer backwards and forwards in your links to stimulate thought – for example; 'If you think back to the diagram before the last ...' or 'See if you can work out how the next picture bears on this', and so on.

For an instant, 'spontaneous' picture, your preparation needs to be even more thorough. When you arrive at your wording, practise drawing as you talk. This is by no means as easy as it sounds. You should also 'script' when to change the colour of your pen. Nothing can be left to chance.

With your script prepared, you must now learn it. Read it through several times to yourself until it has soaked into your consciousness and you can repeat it word for word. When you have mastered the content, move on to emphasis and feelings. Tape-record each section as you read aloud and then listen to the result with the ears of a stranger. This will make you cringe, but persevere. Let your voice move up and down and at different speeds as in normal conversation. Do this repeatedly until you are satisfied that what you have to say is worth listening to and stimulating.

Talking to a tape-recorder should do wonders for your confidence, but you will be talking to an audience, not a machine. This means talking 'out' instead of 'down' and probably at a higher volume level than you have used so far. Take your OHP to your centre for a solo dress-rehearsal. Set out all your materials and equipment exactly as they will be and then go into action as you look at an imaginary audience. Use a pointer as you would in reality and get into the habit of switching the machine off between projections. Keep your back straight, breathe deeply and avoid turning around to the screen.

You are now ready for a full dress-rehearsal. Get friends or family to sit through the presentation, but make it clear that you will be asking for honest comments and reactions afterwards. (If possible, get someone to video you as well.)

The next step is a paying audience!

TURNING ON

Like any other sort of training aid, the OHP needs to be checked and tested before it is used in a session. OHPs, as mentioned earlier, are very dependable and well behaved. If anything does go wrong, then it is generally a job that requires specialist help, except for the following:

1. *Bulb failure*. Some machines carry a back-up lamp and if yours does, you do not have a problem. All you need to do is to flip a switch and carry on with the presentation. If your machine does not have this facility, however, you should familiarise yourself with what goes where – the middle of a darkened room with 20 or 30 expectant faces looking at you is not the place to learn, so practise and be prepared!

   Should you need to replace a bulb, remember that it will be *very hot*. Use a cloth when you take it out.

2. *Fuse failure*. Plug fuses also tend to go at the most inconvenient moment. Sellotape a spare fuse of the appropriate sort to the side of your projector.

Now find yourself a good, solid table to set the OHP on. The slightest tremor will register as a major earthquake, so do pay special attention to this point. There may be occasions when you have to work on an uneven floor, so keep a few beer-mats in your teacher's tool-kit.

If at all possible, have a separate table in an 'L'-shaped arrangement on which to rest transparencies and miscellaneous items; storing them on the edge next to your projector is asking for trouble.

The ideal situation for your OHP may well require the use of an extension cable. As always when using leads, ensure that these are not a danger to yourself or your students.

Check that there are no competing sources of light which might prove a distraction. Although a good OHP does not need darkened conditions to be effective, its impact will be lessened by unwanted illumination. Do whatever you can to shut out the problem.

Set out the chairs and tables for students in the style that you prefer (classroom, horseshoe, etc). You can work from a standing position if you wish, but you will obtain better control by sitting with your back to the screen (see Figure 6.3).

The other advantage to remaining seated is that you avoid casting your own shadow. After going to so much trouble to get a perfect image, it seems a pity to spoil it (see Figure 6.4).

Good presentation

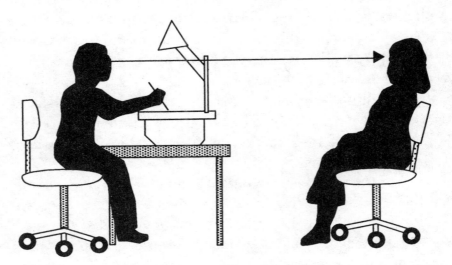

Make sure you project at eye level when in a small group

Figure 6.3

ON SCREEN

Having ensured that your machine is in working order, you need to look for a suitable projection area. At a pinch, this can be a clean section of wall, but investing in a portable screen will mean fewer problems and compromises. Besides offering a smooth, matt white surface, modern portable screens can not only be adjusted for height, but they can also be tilted. This allows the beam to be angled perfectly to give a square image rather than a coffin-box shape (see Figure 6.5 on page 83). The actual size of the projected image is determined by how far or close it is to the surface used; the nearer you are, the smaller the picture will be.

Do not let your shadow obscure the screen

Figure 6.4

REVELATION, MASKING AND OVERLAY

There are a number of simple handling techniques with acetates that can liven up your presentation and in so doing will help your students to remember it all the better.

Revelation at its most basic is covering lines up until you need them. Say, for example, that you have a list of five points about driving behaviour. You could simply show all five points on screen and have done with it, but in so doing you will lose the impact and control of each item. Your students may well have different reading speeds and abilities. One student could be on point five, while another may still be worrying about point one.

Alternatively, imagine that you take the same list but that you keep it covered with a piece of card. As you begin to talk, you slide the card down to reveal point one, which appears out of nowhere to take the audience's attention. You can then elaborate on this item and ask questions until you are sure that the whole group is happy with it, at which point you can move to the next item.

Masking is similar in principle, but is a little more sophisticated. In this technique, a picture, for example, is partly covered up by squares of card which are then removed to reveal the whole.

Overlay adds on rather than removes, as in the previous two techniques. A typical overlay presentation might begin with a clean graph display on to which pictures of vehicles or statistics are added. This presentation is very effective with car parts and mechanics as it allows you to build up an image as you speak.

USING TV, VCR AND CAMCORDERS

The television and its accessories, the video cassette player (VCR) and the camcorder, are now so commonplace that almost everyone knows how they work. As their technology becomes more advanced, the easier they become to operate, with the result that the most recent models are practically idiot-proof. For all that familiarity, however, very few trainers actually know how to *use* them. To most tutors, putting on an 'educational' video is akin to having a tea-break. As the television is switched on, so the attention of the class is switched off as they are left to watch, doodle or sleep as they choose. This is not education but abdication. This is all the more pity since these tools can be so very valuable in a training programme.

At the risk of becoming a bore in order to stop you becoming one, equipment such as television and VCRs are training aids not trainers. This is not to say that straightforward instructional tapes do not have their place in the lecture room. They most certainly do, but that place is not in the teacher's seat. Pause for a moment and think about the situation described above in which a video is simply switched on. A student would not remember everything you said in a 60-minute talk, so why is he or she expected to remember it on screen? Even a magic box has its limitations.

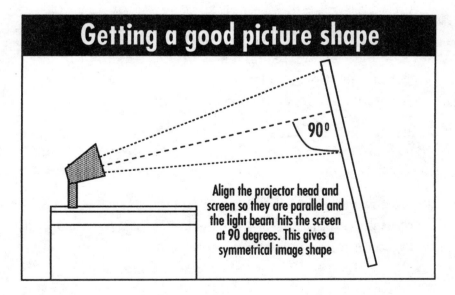

Figure 6.5

HARD FACTS

Although televisions and VCRs can be taken for granted as pieces of equipment, there are a few distinct points to remember in their classroom use:

- When selecting a television, keep in mind the size of the group you intend to work with. Too small a screen will be invisible from the back row.
- Choose a model with a remote control that is easy to operate in dimly lit conditions. Avoid controls with too many buttons or small ones that are hard to find.
- Check the freeze-frame quality before you make your selection.
- Remember that height also plays a part in visibility; you may need a portable office-style stand.
- Poor sound quality will destroy the best presentation; avoid models with a 'tinny' blare.
- Combined TV/VCR units are truly portable, but if either part malfunctions, you are at more of a disadvantage than you are with separate, replaceable items.

Many of the basic rules that apply to other audio-visual aids also apply to televisions and videos, but there are a few other rules to remember:

1. All equipment should be set up and tested well in advance of the arrival of the class. Check all parts from hand- to tape-control. As there are more possible problem areas than with an OHP, you need to be thorough.
2. When you are using a hand-held remote control, be sure that you know its effective range and angle of operation. Standing in front of the class making ineffectual clicks will leave you looking faintly ridiculous.

3. If you are presenting in a room with lights, ensure that reflections or glare do not spoil the images; if you are working in a darkened area, screen out any light creeping under doors and also appoint a monitor to switch the lights on or off at your request.
4. Be very wary of trailing wires. These can cause problems if you lose yourself in your enthusiasm to get on with the show or if students trip over them if they leave the room.
5. Have the videos you intend to use clearly labelled and to hand. Use hard cases rather than cardboard sleeves which quickly become tatty.
6. When you are not using the remote control, keep it pointed downwards. The accidental triggering of a function button can cause anything from mirth to panic!
7. Turn off the set as soon as you have finished using it. If you do need to switch back on, remember that many models have reset levels which can come into life very suddenly and very loudly.
8. If you intend to use the freeze-frame, do *not* talk to the television! Continue to talk to the class.

SOFT OPTIONS

The most difficult part of using audio-visual equipment is the application of the software. As mentioned above, there is a real tendency when using the television and VCRs simply to press the play button and leave the class to watch the programme. You can show video tapes through in their entirety, of course, but you run the risk of losing your students' attention. Regrettably, most educational features are not Hollywood blockbusters that will keep them glued to their seats!

If you want to make the best use of commercially available videos rather than let your class watch them passively, play them in small doses. Allow for ten or so minutes of tape time, then stop the action at a selected point. Ask for feedback or questions from the group and perhaps elaborate on a point on a flip-chart or dry-wipe board. Break off from passive viewing and get into a discussion that makes everyone feel involved. The effect of this will be to enhance the content of the videos and also to extend their 'length'. The same video-tape can thus be a one-off show or an interactive tool to be used over several sessions.

Any commercially purchased video should be watched and studied beforehand by the teacher. First, assess its worth. If it is boring or repetitive, then avoid using it. If it passes your quality test, then think about how you are going to use it to best advantage. What notes or book chapters do you need to tie it in with, what role-plays or games logically follow on? Once again, think about your presentation. Just because someone else is talking, it does not mean that you have nothing to say. (In your reviewing capacity, try to see as many new titles as possible and give them a star rating. Should a student ask you whether or not they should invest in a particular copy, you can then give them valuable guidance.)

Finally, when you are using purchased videos, do pay attention to copyright rules and restrictions. Apart from the legality of your action, you will also be in danger of falling foul of the student who will tell everyone in a very loud voice that you are breaking the law. It is not easy to get the class to take you seriously after that!

Tapes made by companies are not the only options open to you. The miniaturisation of high-quality video-recorders means that, with a little study or training, you can make good educational tapes of your own. Showing these to paying audiences is somewhat different from showing your latest holiday video, however! Before you attempt to do this, you should master the technical aspects of using the camera either through attending a course or by reading books or, indeed, through watching tapes.

Having mastered the techniques for using the camera, you next need to write a script. Write down what you want to say and how you want to say it. Keep the text short and simple, and avoid big or technical terms unless you intend to explain them. Ensure that any actors you intend to use are presentable and not unintentionally humorous. If you cannot train them to avoid their own verbal idiosyncrasies, then choose some alternatives quickly. This advice applies to your own vocabulary and verbal habits.

VARIOUS VIDEOS

Having mastered your basic audio-visual technique, you can now begin to explore some of the styles that are open to you. It is a big mistake to think that all videos are the same in purpose and use. Using a variety of tapes that are suited to different situations will make your teaching more effective and more fun.

Trigger videos

Trigger videos are easy to make instructional tools as they have an impact that is entirely out of proportion to their length. Like any video-tape, they demand and attract the viewers' attention. What makes them so special is that those watching them have to get involved for real.

A trigger video is a brief sequence designed to provoke a response. Teacher and pupil, or just a pupil, are shown in a driving situation that could become dangerous or problematic. The video is stopped abruptly and the student(s) are asked to talk through what should happen next.

Trigger videos can really liven up a training session, especially when they concern situations with an emotional content – for example, you have just got involved in a dispute over parking with another motorist: what are you going to do? Depending on the subject, these videos can be extremely short and are sometimes all the more powerful for it.

Quiz videos

For this exercise, film a short driving procedure that relates to the theory questions that have been studied but add numerous deliberate mistakes. Ask the students to watch the tape and to write down any errors they spot. As with trigger videos, their answers can then be used to broaden out into a discussion or role-play.

After looking at a film showing many driving errors, it is important that students should see a video straight afterwards illustrating the correct procedure. This applies even when the students have registered high scores in their observation of the errors. The image that they have last seen will be the one that they remember.

THE ELECTRIC CAMP-FIRE

Hundreds and thousands of years ago, people would gather at night around a fire and talk, laugh, sing or tell stories as they watched the flickering tongues of flame lap and crackle.

Today, although the world has become computerised, human beings still have the same basic urges and needs. However, we now have an electronic camp-fire: it's called television.

Very few people actually *watch* television: 90 per cent of our viewing time is devoted to chatter or ridicule as we attack the behaviour of others from a safe distance. We criticise our nearest and dearest at secondhand, or tell each other horror stories based on what we see. Sometimes we just have the television on as a source of colour and noise.

You can utilise this modern fact of life in your training. When confronted by a television set and video-recorder, most students become passive, waiting to be instructed and spoon-fed with varying degrees of enthusiasm.

There is an alternative method. First, equipped with a cam-corder, go out and film 20 or 30 minutes of everyday road behaviour. You might need to do a few 'takes', but you will soon have a fine collection of bad motoring habits. Then, sur-prise your students by playing the tape to them and asking them for feedback, jokes, warnings, etc. during the show. Students will soon get the idea and the session will take on a life of its own. In the background, you can act as a village elder, transmitting attitudes, responses and manners in a way that no book can ever provide. (In the first instance, though, warn your students that there is no dramatic conclusion or high-speed chase. Tell them that what you are offering is a glimpse of normal, everyday life from which they can learn.)

TAPED DISCUSSIONS

Taping class discussions or role-plays can be a useful exer-cise. These can be played back at a later stage to illustrate a change in attitude or perception. Once removed, they can also be played to other groups as raw material for their own course-work.

TAPED TUTORIALS

If you feel really confident and capable with your teaching, you can even film yourself in action. The resulting tape, which can have in-built tasks or study breaks – for example, 'Now read Chapter 7' or 'Answer the following questions' – can then be loaned to students or played in your absence or sickness by someone else.

END CREDITS

Mastering the techniques required to make your own videos will take some time and effort, but the rewards are great. Self-made tapes have no copyright problems and cost little. More importantly, however, they are customised to your own training programme, and offer variety, stimulation and involvement.

'VIDEO NASTIES'

In connection with the use of television and VCRs, the following is a selection of rules that are worth remembering:

- Do not let the tape run without watching for signs of boredom in your audience. If you see people getting restless or yawning, move in swiftly to change the situation.

- At the opposite extreme, avoid overusing the freeze-frame button.
- Play from 'cold'. Several seconds of a popular soap or the news played as you fiddle with the tape will ruin the session.
- Do not have the television playing as you talk.
- Turn the volume up *slowly*.
- Do not talk to the television or turn your back on the audience. Sitting 'in' the group may feel comfortable, but it is asking for trouble.

SLIDE PROJECTORS

Prior to the arrival of cheap video equipment, the slide projector was *the* educational tool for showing brightly coloured images to students. Nowadays, slide projectors have declined in importance, but, used correctly, they can still be useful.

Modern slide projectors come complete with remote-control units, which theoretically remove the need for an assistant. Some, too, offer a sound facility by which means a tape is played alongside the image. These are fine, but a word of warning is given here. Slide projectors are more likely to fail to operate than all the other pieces of audio-visual equipment put together. Because they have moving parts that jam or stick, they can be a real nuisance. Familiarity with the machine, therefore, is absolutely essential.

Finally, as with all the other equipment, you need a good, lively script that does not sound like a script. A boring talk with on/off images in a darkened room will send your audience to sleep.

SLIDE VIEWERS

These pieces of equipment have much the same use as slide projectors, but they operate on a much smaller scale. At one end of the price and size range are desk-top executive models capable of presenting a full show; at the other end are cheap battery-powered versions offering just one image at a time.

Slide viewers allow for a less formal audio-visual present-ation. They also eliminate the need for a screen, with all the fuss and expense this implies.

Desk-top viewers (which also work as projectors) are best used with groups of four to eight students who are encour-aged to gather around them in a relaxed huddle, allowing the ADI to speak in a more natural fashion.

The smaller types of viewers used by photography enthu-siasts can also have a place in training. A key slide is inserted, and the viewer and its sharp little image is passed around from student to student. Alternatively, the viewer can be used in a theory circuit, whereby students are asked to answer a question or to offer a comment.

7

MISCELLANEOUS TRAINING AIDS

OVERVIEW

Despite the fact that we live in a world of hi-tech equipment where everything we own seems to bleep, squawk or talk, there are still training aids that manage to function without batteries. Books and boards were used to help develop minds long before OHPs or videos ever saw the light of day, and they achieved some remarkable results. The secret of effective training aids rests not with the tools themselves but with their users.

When using training aids of any sort, try to keep in mind the example of an actor and his or her props. An actor may wield a sword or wave a pan, but the audience is never forgotten. Do not talk to flip-charts, screens or whatever – talk to your students! That way the training aid will be a training aid and not a cover for your emotional nakedness as you stand in front of a wide-eyed group of students.

The following items are cheap, effective and usable by any ADI, whatever his or her background. Practise using each one in dry runs until it feels natural, then apply. Keep the number of aids employed per session strictly rationed – your aim is to educate, not dazzle.

FLIP-CHARTS

Anyone who has ever sat through a training session is more than likely to be familiar with flip-charts. Usually fixed to a portable frame, they can be used to:

- Demonstrate pre-prepared material.
- Record the thoughts of the group.

They are relatively cheap, cheerful and easy to use. If you can't afford or object to an OHP, then thoroughly master your flip-chart technique.

Many of the principles that apply to OHP transparencies also apply to preparing flip-chart pages. Keep your message for each page simple and direct, leaving good spaces between the lines. Before you start to ruin a brand new chart, practise your layout and technique on the back of a roll of unwanted wallpaper. Check and double-check all spellings and factual information; a glaring error will both distract attention and deal a blow to your credibility. Ensure that lines are straight by ruling in pencil guiders which you can erase later.

Whatever words you do decide upon, the letters themselves need to be about 50mm in height – this should make them comfortably visible from a distance of up to 9m. The gaps in between the lines, which need to be around 60mm, have other applications besides keeping things tidy. You can write in pencil key words or phrases as prompts. Visible only to yourself, these will help out greatly should you dry up in the middle of a presentation.

Select the markers you intend to use with care. Choose broad-tipped ones with bright and contrasting colours, avoiding paler shades which will be hard to see from the back.

With the chart prepared, you are now in a position to build a script around it. Use one A4 page per flip-chart page to record any jokes or comments you might want to make about the subject in hand. The next stage is to memorise the words and then to recite them aloud to yourself. Do this until you feel completely natural and that you are talking rather than reciting. When you have arrived at this point, you are ready for a dress rehearsal.

Ask your partner or some friends to act as students and then carry out the presentation *exactly* as you would for real. On this basis, 'arrive' early to set up and check your equipment. Having such an established pattern will help you to overcome many basic errors, such as dry pens or standing at the wrong height. It will also help you to overcome last-minute nerves.

Check that the markers you intend to use work. Your audience may find it funny if they don't, but you most certainly will not! Have spares available just in case and keep them in the pen-tray that most easels have. The flip-chart cover should be down as your students enter to allow for maximum visual impact when you do go to work.

For the purpose of your simulation, resort to the TTT theorem – *tell* your audience what you are going to tell them, *tell* them, and then *tell* them what you have told them. Spend a minute or so putting people at ease and then turn over the flip-chart cover to reveal your title page. It is at this point that many trainers forget that they have an audience. It cannot be stressed too often that you must *not* talk to the visual aids but to your students. Use a transparent ruler to act as a pointer, holding it on the line you are dealing with only as long as it is required. (Laser pointers are also highly effective if you can afford one.)

Turn over each sheet the moment you have dealt with it. Some chart pages have a tendency to tumble back to leave you looking foolish. This can be avoided by fixing a piece of double-sided adhesive tape or Blu-Tack to the bottom. Press as you turn over in one smooth, firm movement.

As soon as you have finished speaking, close the show down with the cover. Any writing or figures that remain visible will draw the attention away from you and disturb the next phase of the lesson.

Pre-prepared charts of this kind can be used a number of times if they are handled carefully: store them flat or in cardboard tubes. Even after they have become a little tatty, they can be pressed into service as hangings on the classroom walls.

The same basic principles apply when you are using an empty pad. Again, rule in faint lines to keep your writing straight and controlled. Hold pens with the point down as you write to ensure a good flow of ink. And talk to your students!

WHITEBOARDS

Even more of a bargain is a flip-chart easel with a dry-wipe whiteboard surface. This allows for other types of work such as brain-storming at a lower cost.

The only other tool that is required in addition to the flip-chart, is a soft cloth to wipe the board as you deliver an explanation or at the finish of the session. Keep the pen pointing downwards as you write and replace the cap as soon as you stop using it.

If, during the course of the session, an idea or phrase is thrown up that sounds impressive, write it down in your notebook. The real benefit of using a whiteboard or flip-chart is that each week you will have a group of different minds tackling the same subjects. Learn to learn from your students.

TEXTBOOKS

You should always bring a full set of relevant textbooks to every group session. HMSO publications such as *Your Theory Driving Test*, *The Driving Manual*, etc are essential, but you should also try to have other titles available on topics such as first aid, basic repairs, etc. A stack of volumes by the desk will do wonders for both your self-confidence and your image!

All students should be encouraged to bring their own personal copy of the *Highway Code* and *The Driving Manual* with them to every class. Not all students will, of course, so you should have a few well-thumbed copies available for passing around the class, and a few pristine ones for sale. The income you derive from this will be small, but it adds to the profitability of your theory work.

Try to avoid working through key sections of *The Driving Manual* or just telling students to read it before the next session. These are the quickest and most effective methods of making anyone hate a book, thus defeating the object of the exercise. Your aim is not only to get people through the test, but to modify their attitude for good.

A method of getting some fun into the use of textbooks is to announce a competition 'spontaneously'. Divide the group into two or more teams and give them both a couple of chapters from which to devise questions (the trickier the better; questions could also include drawn diagrams). Allow about 15 minutes for this exercise and then act as a quiz master. You should expect, and be prepared, for differences of opinion and interpretation. These in turn can be used to stress the need for true understanding as distinct from learning parrot fashion.

Finally, avoid loaning books to students 'just until the next lesson'. You may well get them back, but there is always the possibility that you will not – you have been warned!

NEWSPAPERS

Newspapers are cheap and effective (if unlikely) training aids that can be used in several ways.

For group presentations, collect details of any road accidents or injuries over, say, a week or a month. These can then be used in conjunction with an OHP or flip-chart, or put together in a hand-out. Using a local paper adds real emphasis but be aware that those involved in the incidents may be known to members of the class. Avoid jokes or scathing comments – simply present the facts and let them speak for themselves.

Another part of a newspaper that can be of value is that described by court proceedings. Here you will find listed people who are guilty of various traffic offences together with details of their fines. These can be the basis for discussion and role-play, but again, avoid making jokes or unpleasant comments about the people involved.

The other way of using newspapers is to ask each student to cut out reported road incidents between sessions. This self-discovery method really emphasises the facts and figures.

HAND-OUTS

Hand-outs can be created or bought directly off the shelf. Rather than have students frantically scribbling notes in the traditional, time-honoured (but largely inefficient) manner, talk through your subject and then provide an information sheet. In this way the student is paying attention to you instead of trying to make notes which will most probably be indecipherable later anyway.

Hand-outs should be no more than a page or so in length. Bullet points are the best layout because:

- They capture the attention.
- They are more easily remembered.
- They discourage waffle.

Brevity is everything; the sheets are intended to supplement your instruction, not to replace it. Ensure that each bullet point is no more than a sentence long. This may take a little practice, but persevere until you can convey essential details without wasted words.

Diagrams are also a useful aid in training. A very effective approach is to hand out pictures which require the student to add labels or captions.

Those with access to a personal computer (PC) will have no difficulty in creating a series of working notes for every stage of their training. Those who lack a computer need not despair. You should type up master copies and then keep them in a presentation file with transparent wallets and copy them prior to each session for use as hand-outs. They may not look as fancy, but they will do the job just as well.

CLIPPINGS FILE

It is a good idea to store magazine and newspaper pieces about driving-related matters in a presentation file. Ask friends, family or colleagues to look out for such items for you and within weeks you will have a collection of stories ranging from the funny to the tragic, the interesting to the bizarre. These can then be used for hand-outs, throw-away parting lines, or as the starting point for a discussion.

COLLECTIVE NOTEBOOKS

A simple exercise book, with a little imagination, can become an effective training resource. The idea behind the collective notebook is to set out a problem and to ask a group member to comment with words, pictures or even a newspaper cutting. He or she then passes the book on to the next member, and so on, until it is returned to the tutor. At this point, the various contributions are discussed and analysed.

Collective notebooks are best used with tightly knit groups who see each other on a regular basis – for example, students and employees. Try to make sure that the questions used require thought and opinion, not just a 'yes' or 'no'.

STUDY PACKS

Study packs based on real-life accidents or situations can be bought from specialised shops, as can most of the items in this chapter. Ideal for sessions in which the group is divided into smaller, discovery and discussion-led teams, they really make the student think – and that is the point of any good training aid.

Study packs usually contain photographs, diagrams and prompts, so are very useful to the ADI who is lacking in confidence or presentation skills. They are excellent warm-up tools for role-play; at the most basic level, you can simply take over the situation which is depicted and let the students talk about their feelings.

FLASH CARDS

Flash cards have road symbols or questions on one side and a caption or answer on the other. They can be used in a variety of ways, depending on the group's needs and mood. Firstly, the cards can be held up by the class leader, the students being asked to write down an answer or give a verbal reply. Secondly, they can be adapted to card games, such as snap or poker, with the players trying to catch each other out.

SHOWBOARDS/EXHIBITION STANDS

Essentially glorified folding screens, these aids have applications in both training and sales.

A selection of photographs, diagrams and questions make the stands a useful 'station' in a theory circuit. Alternatively, they can be placed at the back of the training centre to serve as a focal point at coffee-breaks. Advertise your own on-going and specialist services (night driving, advanced driving, etc) in between the other material to emphasise your life-skills approach. Short courses sell especially well this way, as group members encourage each other to enrol for a variety of reasons.

These stands can be hideously expensive to buy new, so do look around for second-hand ones. The DIY enthusiast, on the other hand, may wish to create his or her own.

LEAFLETS

A wide range of leaflets on driving-related matters is available from organisations such as the Royal Society for the Prevention of Accidents (RoSPA) or local safety offices, some of which are free. Leaflets can be distributed, used for project work or kept in a presentation file according to your preferred way of working.

AUDIO CASSETTES

Tapes featuring theory material can be bought from specialist ADI shops or, more laboriously, put together at home. These are usually sold to students, who can play them in their spare time.

Tapes based on questions and answers from the *Highway Code* can also be played to groups if it is thought that a change of voice might benefit the class.

At a pinch, tapes can be used to cover for an ADI who is away sick and a less experienced partner offers to take the class.

COMPUTERS AND COMPUTER PROGRAMMES

Love them or loathe them, computers are a fact of life, and they have found a place for themselves in almost every field of human activity. Driving is no exception to this rule. Theory Test programmes and car simulations are already on the market, and doubtless many more will follow as hi-tech equipment becomes commonplace.

Computers, then, may be used when the ADI is working with small groups of no more than three or four students. This approach works best with younger learners who are more likely to be at ease with computers. (Those who own a PC will probably buy their own discs and dispense with the tutor altogether.)

The driving school of tomorrow will probably own rows of computers – Colleges of Further Education are particularly well equipped to move in this direction. In so far as this extends and encourages the learning process, such an advance is to be welcomed, but few ADIs are likely to be able to afford the necessary investment in equipment.

On a more immediate and mundane level, though, computers can be used to design and store all sorts of test papers, hand-outs and forms.

STEERING-WHEEL TRAINERS

Steering-wheel trainers have often provoked fits of mirth among purists, but they can be very useful in the transition between classroom and car. Offering a degree of resistance, these very basic simulators can be fixed to walls or placed in laps so that students can practise the technique of using a real steering wheel.

The main drawback of using such devices is the problem of supply and demand. One wheel shared between many students can be more of a distraction than an aid! In such a situation, make the wheel a 'station' in a theory circuit.

MAGNETIC BOARDS

These are steel boards on to which magnetic overlays and vehicles can be placed. Often used in cars, they can also work well in group sessions, where the opportunity for students to come to the front and huddle around the board can ease tension and provide a change of pace.

Magnetic boards can also be used like steering-wheel trainers as part of a theory circuit.

MODELS/CAR PARTS

Models of car parts or car parts themselves can add variety to training and can help to make concepts and principles more immediate. Ones with working parts obviously provide the best visual stimulation, but size, portability and cost must play a part in the selection process.

The use of models and car parts naturally leads to dedicated pre- or post-test sessions on basic car maintenance. Such work is of economic benefit to the student, who can save money, and to the ADI, who can earn money, but, more importantly, it can act as the springboard for the kind of lifelong relationship you are trying to encourage with your students.

8

ROLE-PLAYS, GAMES AND EXERCISES

THE GAMES PEOPLE PLAY

The brilliant Dutch scholar Johan Huizinga invented a new name for Mankind. Scientists refer to human beings as *Homo sapiens* – Man the wise – but Huizinga had a different idea regarding what we are all about. He called us *Homo ludens* – Man the game player. In Huizinga's opinion, culture, courtship, law, religion – in short, everything we call human behaviour – springs from the need to play. Animals, he argued, learn how to cope with both the world and other members of their own species through play and we clever apes are no exception. The theory has much to recommend it. When you take a step back and reflect on human activities such as money, government, and so on, you realise that they resemble silly games. We start our life by playing games and leave it in one played out on our behalf.

Games and play have always been important, but it is only over the last few decades that they have found a place in adult education. Nowadays, the use of games is commonplace in training and is almost expected. At one end of the scale are board or card games which are designed to educate students through fun; at the other end, are role-playing games which are designed to help students to explore their feelings or situations. The ADI who wants to succeed in theory tuition should master, or at least be familiar with, all of these types of games.

It is useful for students to learn games in group sessions because:

1. They encourage involvement.
2. They are different and exciting.
3. They present the same necessary information but in a different package.
4. They require no special equipment.
5. They are good ice-breakers and antidotes for nerves or mid-term blues.
6. They can allow students to experience situations that would otherwise be dangerous.
7. They are fun.

There is, of course, a down side to playing games. Older students can regard them as trivial and childish; younger students may reject them because they are 'too much like school'. Then again, they can easily degenerate into horseplay and be a complete waste of time. Whether they are a waste of time or not rests with the skill of the ADI in running them and, in the first instance, in selling the idea of the need for them.

Before suggesting any of the games that follow, the ADI should first explain to the class why they will help. If resistance or scepticism is met, offer the students a glimpse of what they are going to achieve. Isn't the practical driving test a sort of role-playing game? After that, any resistance to or scepticism about games will disappear from most students' minds.

ROLE-PLAY

In a role-play, the members of a group are asked to be themselves or someone else in a particular situation. Each member is then asked to react as he, she or the character portrayed would to unfolding events. Unlike a stage play, no thought is given to the onlookers. The emphasis is on what the group members feel and experience about themselves in that setting.

Role-play is perhaps one of the most useful educational tools that is available to the ADI who is venturing into theory work. Its importance rests on its ability to change and shape attitudes, to help the individual to *understand* rather than just to *learn*. The simple repetition of facts will never make anyone a more careful or considerate driver. Take as a random example the rules on alcohol consumption and driving. Everyone knows that they should not drink and drive, and as from July 1996 candidates who have prepared for the Theory Test will be able to cite safe blood levels with regard to alcohol consumption. Is that information, then, going to make them say 'no' to a drink when they are out with the car?

The sad answer to the above question is not likely to be in the affirmative, despite millions of pounds' worth of publicity and countless warnings. Is one to conclude that people who ignore such warnings are monsters or criminals? The answer to that, too, is in the negative. Most of those involved are decent individuals who would not wish to kill or maim another human being. Scarcely one person in a thousand would argue that it is a sensible thing to get behind the wheel after a few drinks, yet many drivers do.

The problem is to be found in the difference between known and understood information. If the same driver had experienced the endless guilt caused by a drink-driving accident, the enduring shame of having his or her name announced on the television and in the newspapers, felt the pain caused by injury, would he or she think twice about drinking and driving? This time the answer probably is 'yes'. Unfortunately, few people ever live through such an experience to understand its emotional and practical consequences. There is, however, a safe short-cut. It's called role-play.

PLAYTIME: RUNNING THE ROLE-PLAY

It would be certain death, of course, for you to turn up at a training session one week and to announce casually that you are going to run a role-play. Even assuming that you are fully prepared for it, few of your students will be. Their shyness will bubble quickly into frustration and anger, with the result that the class may be somewhat light in numbers for the next few weeks.

If you are going to use role-play, you should touch upon it in your preview talk or syllabus; this gives those who are seriously troubled by it the chance to decline without losing face. For the rest, the topic should be reintroduced after a few 'proper' sessions when the students are possibly becoming tired of theory work. Just prior to the end of the class, explain that you have something very different in mind for the next week. Sweeten the pill by referring to the benefits of the exercise in terms of passing the Theory and Practical driving tests and leave it at that.

The best way to arrive at a role-playing situation is to let it evolve. Just as our bodies need to be warmed up before engaging in sport, so the mind and emotions need to be made ready before a new kind of activity. Start the session with case histories and discussion, then move on to role-playing games and the role-play itself.

In actual practice, the session might go something like this. Let's say that the chosen subject for the role-play is how to stop peer pressure causing students to drink and drive (see Appendix 2). After the initial welcome and housekeeping items, open the show with a stark, chilling OHP/flip-chart presentation. Deal with cold statistics; the emotions bringing them to life will be supplied later in the proceedings.

Move swiftly into a brain-storming exercise. Ask the class why so many people choose to drink and drive when they know the risks and penalties. Try to get everyone used to talking and help those students who seem a little shy by the practice of sentence filling. (Take their key idea and expand it, going back to them to check it fully.)

The next stage (which can be skipped if the group is talkative and relaxed) is to provide a further chance to relax with a case study. Use a pack or, better still, devise one of your own around the eventual role-play. As an example, present a situation in which a non-fatal accident has occurred: the driver responsible was returning from an office leaving party where he or she had a few drinks. Stress that only a few drinks were involved – making the driver totally drunk will defeat the object of the exercise. The student needs to be identified with someone like him- or herself facing a not uncommon temptation. Divide the class into smaller groups and ask each to elect a spokesperson. Suggest the direction you want things to move in by asking the groups to consider the ways in which the driver could have avoided the 'one for the road' without giving offence. Allow about seven or eight minutes for this, during which time you can wander around to give help, advice and discipline as required.

Now everyone should be brought back together for what is a crucial phase in the role-play. At this point the report must be turned into a graduated lead into what is to come. Human behaviour will give you a head-start in this task. Those students who were elected as spokespersons will normally be talkative, outgoing and willing to try something new – just the sort you need as volunteers. You will not be asking for volunteers, however, as that would be clumsy and likely to upset people. What you are going to do is to engage these naturally talkative show-offs in a conversation that is almost a role-play in itself.

Ask the first of your spokespersons what his or her group felt that the driver could have done. Near the end of the report, turn to one of the other students and ask him or her what they might feel if they were the victim of such a motorist:

ADI:	Dave, if I could stop you there for a second. Liz, let's say you happened to be the other driver in this case. Dave's just smashed into your nice new BMW with added extras. How do you feel about that?
Liz:	Pig sick! I'd brain him!
ADI:	I'll bet. Now, though, he comes over to apologise and provide his details. It's then that you smell the lager. How are you feeling now?
Liz:	Very, *very* angry. I'd get the police.
ADI:	But Dave's admitted it's his fault. He says he'll pay.
Liz:	Oh, he'll pay all right! He should lose his licence and everything.
ADI:	He's never had an accident in his life, though, Liz, not in 15 years' driving. Don't you think you're being a bit mean?
Liz:	He shouldn't be driving. He could have killed me!

ADI:	Thanks, Liz. How are you feeling about this, Dave?
Dave:	A bit of a prat!
ADI:	Do you feel she's got a point?
Dave:	I can understand it, but …
ADI:	You're a rep aren't you, Dave? If she makes a fuss, how do you think your boss will feel?
Dave:	He will not be a happy man.
ADI:	Could you do your job without a car?
Dave:	Not really.

The dialogue is, of course, imaginary, but if things go according to plan, it will go surprisingly like this example. Now that the group leaders are involved, you need to bring in the rest of the students. Get feedback about the rights and wrongs of the situation. Collect thoughts and ideas and then refocus:

ADI:	Dave, we know you're normally a responsible driver. Why did you take the drink?
Dave:	Well, I'd had a big meal and I wasn't driving far.
ADI:	But you could have said no?
Dave:	Somebody bought me it, so …
ADI:	Maybe people were putting pressure on you to be one of the gang?
Dave:	Something like that.

Leaving Dave alone, draw the rest of the group in. Depending on the class size, you can split into smaller units or work as one. Choosing more talkative members again, set the scene. Everyone is back in the restaurant and it's almost time to go. Our nominated drivers are going to have to make a decision. The rest of the group has to coerce them into taking one for the road by any number of pleas, jokes or sarcastic comments. The driver, on his or her part, cannot leave nor risk offending the group. What's going to happen?

At this point you should be able to offer players readymade roles that they can slip on like coats. Present in the group, for instance, could be members from the next office our driver wants to get in with, a girl he wants to impress, and so on. Ask the players to react how they think that person would do in real life.

Let the role-play run for a while, adding your own comments from time to time if necessary. When the situation seems fully explored, call time and give the students a few moments to chat and laugh.

The role-play session ends with a debriefing. This is a very serious business and needs to be dealt with as such. Unless you follow the exercise through, the role-play will have been just a game with limited value. Ask the players what they felt, what they discovered. How did it feel to be on the receiving end of all those jokes? Why did they want the driver to take a drink? What means are there to escape from such a situation?

Running a role-play is by no means as strange or as difficult as it might sound. Anyone can do it, provided they fully understand the principles and are fully prepared.

KIM'S GAME

This little entertainment was devised by Rudyard Kipling for his novel *Kim*, hence the name. It can be used as an icebreaker, a mental warm-up routine or as a straightforward test of observation.

An assortment of 30 or so different objects are placed on

a tray and covered with a cloth by the ADI. This is then removed by the ADI for 30 seconds and then replaced, at which time the students are asked to write down as many items as they can remember. The objects used can be varied from week to week or left the same to make a point. This is a very useful method of helping those who believe they have a poor memory to gain confidence.

CRASH-TEST DUMMIES

Dummies do more than just drive cars into walls for vehicle manufacturers. You can see real-life examples driving around every day making phone calls, eating, smooching, watching TV – in short, doing anything except behaving with due care and attention!

This observational game can be played outside the class and acts as a link between lessons. Ask students, as they wait at bus-stops or wherever, to watch for careless, mindless people sitting behind the wheel of a car. Any really memorable examples should be shared and laughed over as you draw some serious conclusions.

A, B, C

Another fun game that can act as a warm-up or diversion is played along similar lines to musical chairs. Make three large cards marked A, B and C, then place them as far apart as possible around the training room. Read out multiple-choice questions from the Driving Standards Agency (DSA) answer bank and tell the players to stand on the card which represents the correct answer. Players must respond instantly and remain by the card of their first choice. If their choice is incorrect, they are eliminated; if not, they go on to the next question. The procedure is repeated until no players are left or 30 questions are exhausted.

This game is useful in encouraging quick decisions, self-reliance and freedom from group behaviour.

PENALTY POINTS

A useful game that uses bids can be constructed around the penalty-points system. Divide the class into two teams and appoint a captain for each. Read out questions that involve driving offences and the licence points that each attracts. A correct bid or answer wins a point, a miss scores nothing. Work through 20 or 30 questions and save a really difficult one as a tie-breaker should it be required.

Vary the delivery of your questions and inject a little humour – for example, 'Would a motorist caught driving with defective eyesight get three points, six points or a pre-scription for a new pair of bifocals? Team A, your bid.' Watch TV shows and draw your inspiration from them. Observing how a professional personality handles an audience and analysing what happens is an educational experience.

COSTS

Pen and paper are required for this game. Ask students to write down the figure they expect to pay in total for theory and driving tuition at the top of a sheet of paper. Next read out a variety of costs that might result from short-cutting the learning process by reducing or skipping lessons. For instance, you could ask how much it will cost to fail the Theory Test or how much extra in bus or train fares the delay will cost. Move on then to more thought-provoking questions such as the cost of an accident. Each figure needs to be written below the cost of tuition and set against it.

This exercise really drives home the cost of cheap solutions and should encourage students to stay with you for the distance. It can also be used when you are selling yourself at a seminar or group talk. The point to make is that the cheapest isn't always the best.

'DIRECTIONS'

If you have ever found yourself frustrated by directions such as 'Go left, right?', then you will probably know just how to play this game. Ask the group to stand in a relaxed position in an open space and tell them that they are to move around in a circle, keeping a reasonable distance apart. As they move, you will call out various commands which they must follow exactly and instantly. Begin with very simple instructions such as 'turn left' or 'reverse' and then progress to more ambiguous ones. Soon people will end up colliding with each other in fits of laughter, but you will have made your point – that the motorist must use his or her brain rather than just act blindly.

You can position chairs and cut-out cardboard road-signs to further liven things up if you feel so inclined.

CATCH AND CALL

This game illustrates in a most effective way how reducing nervous tension can help to improve hand and eye co-ordination. Begin by picking up a tennis ball and ask for a volunteer who considers him- or herself really bad at catching a ball. When your laughing, nervous victim appears, toss them the ball in a very slow, deliberate fashion and get them to throw it back to you. Now repeat the process, but talk at the same time. Ask the student their name, about their job, and so on. As you do this, stealthily increase the speed of your throws. In nine cases out of ten, the 'hopeless' catcher, distracted from fears and worries, will end up throwing the ball around with a speed they thought impossible.

Students can also play this game in pairs. Follow through the exercise with a discussion about how they can apply this discovery in other learning situations.

THEORY CIRCUIT

A useful antidote to boredom is to wrap up theory training in another form. Those familiar with sports will recognise what follows as an adaptation of something called 'circuit training' in which the participant has to undertake certain exercises or use pieces of equipment in a non-stop chase until he or she has finished the course.

Set out chairs and tables around your training centre and on each put something to be done that requires a few minutes' attention. This could be answering ten questions, identifying ten road symbols, and so on. Use any pieces of equipment you have, such as whiteboards, slide viewers, etc, so that each 'station', as it is known, has a different feel to it. Show the students where to start, then leave them to their own devices.

MOCK EXAMINATIONS

These fall midway between normal training practice and role-play. When the ADI puts students through such examinations, he or she should try to make them every bit as intimidating as the real experience.

Announce the mock examination several weeks in advance to build up pressure and nerves. If it can be arranged at the same time as the actual test in your area, so much the better. If not, there are various steps you can take to increase the pressure.

The first measure you can take is to change location from the comfortable and the familiar. For small groups, it might be possible to conduct the examination in your local library or reference library. Sit the students down with paper and pencil, then issue the tests. Observe the rules as fully as in the real examination and disqualify anyone who talks or leaves the room. (Accompanying them to the toilet will not do anything for your reputation, so forget that particular rule.)

A second method of creating discomfort is to have a friend or partner act as the examiner. Stern expressions and hushed tones are the only qualities required – you will do the marking. If you do not have a friend or partner to stand in for you, arrive in a tie and suit so that you look official.

BRAIN-STORMING

'Brain-storming' is a form of group work that is ideal for starting a session or leading into a role-play. The ADI stands by the flip-chart/board and proposes a question or situation which requires thought. To avoid a sea of blank faces, suggest a few 'for instances' and write them down. Go around the group in turn, but also ask for spontaneous ideas. The aim is to provoke and stimulate; there are no 'correct' answers.

As an example, imagine a brain-storm that is built around a situation where the car in front has just run over a dog. Some replies to your question 'What would you do in such a situation?' might include:

- Brake before I hit the car.
- Call the police.
- Drive off and pretend you didn't notice.
- Run it over again to make sure it's dead.

Take anything that comes without making a comment at this stage. When the group has exhausted itself, pick out the more useful points for discussion.

Try to select topics that are not too black-and-white – situations are rarely that simple on the road.

BREATHING EXERCISES

A simple and not-too-obvious breathing exercise routine can be taught to help students who suffer badly from pre-examination nerves.

When we find ourselves in danger or under stress, our bodies prepare us against the consequences. Blood drains from our faces, our heart rate increases and breathing becomes more rapid and shallow in what is called the 'fight or flight response'. Our emotions and thoughts, then, can influence our bodies, and the reverse is also true. This simple fact is the central principle of breath control and breathing exercises practised by many Eastern mind/body disciplines.

Just as shallow, fast breathing is a symptom of fear, slow and controlled breathing is linked to calm, restful states. Very few people these days breathe to anything like their full capacity, and this in itself can bring about some real mind changes.

Take students through the following exercise. Ask them to place a thumb over one nostril so that it is effectively closed. They then breathe in very slowly, filling their lungs from the bottom upwards. The image to keep in front of them is that of pouring in a jug of water that will fill up the very last centimetre of lung space.

When the students feel full to bursting, tell them to reposition their hand so that both nostrils are sealed. At this point they should hold their breath for a few seconds, then release the nostril they closed first. The air that they have stored is then released in a deep but controlled exhalation. This must not be a gasp, but a slow, deliberate motion. When the lungs are empty the process is repeated with the opposite nostril closed, and then repeated several times.

A few rounds of this exercise will really steady the nerves. With a little practice, it becomes an inconspicuous gesture even when seated at a desk. (No one is likely to notice a student practising this exercise prior to the start of the examination anyway.)

VISUALISATION EXERCISES

Visualisation – that is, controlled day-dreaming about a particular subject or set of circumstances – finds its best use in the practical phase of training, but there are good reasons for introducing it into the syllabus at an early stage. Chief among these reasons is the matter of student motivation. Very few students see theory work as desirable in itself, regarding it as more of an infringement of their right to drive. The sullen resentment which this breeds consigns theory that has been learned by rote to the waste-paper bin along with hated school subjects. Visualisation helps theory to stick in the memory by keeping the long-term goal of driving literally in the mind's eye.

The art of visualisation is to imagine oneself *completely* in a given situation. An exercise might begin with the student seeing him- or herself getting into the car, touching the wheel, smelling the seats, and so on prior to visualising the routine itself. The more intense the dream, the greater is its power to effect change. When the mind has been in this state for a while, it can no longer distinguish fantasy from reality, and then real learning can take place. (There is a famous story about a high-jumper who was caught lazing in a hammock one day. When asked why he wasn't training, he opened one eye and said that he was. In fact, he was seeing himself go through the steps of his run-up, imagining how he needed to thrust himself upwards, feeling how he would twist his body in the actual event.)

Visualisation is a sort of role-play for one and it shares many advantages with that form of training. Situations which in real life might be difficult or dangerous can be experienced second-hand. If the drills are done sufficiently well and often enough, they can prepare the student to react in the required manner. Also, like role-play, the technique needs no special equipment or skill.

With a little imagination on your part, a series of visualisations can be put together for all sorts of learning experiences. Decide upon your objective and then break it down, step by step, like a film director numbering scenes. Write out a script in detail, then, telling your students to close their eyes, talk them through the situation. Speak slow, low and soft, providing mental 'pegs' on which they can hang their own images.

9

HELPING DEMOTIVATED STUDENTS

REACTIONS TO FAILURE

Any examination carries with it the possibility of failure and the Theory Driving Test is no exception to this rule. It is estimated that perhaps 25–30 per cent of candidates will not get through their first attempt at the test, and among these figures will be individuals who fail repeatedly. The ADI, of course, is well accustomed to dealing with the emotional consequences of poor performance, and it might be argued that the treatment for a Theory Driving Test failure need be no different from that offered for a practical failure – that is, encouragement, repetition and a resit. In reality, however, there are a number of important reasons why the approach needs to be different, especially where multiple failures are involved.

The first thing to remember when dealing with multiple-failure candidates is that the Theory Test is perceived to be 'easy'. Most people will pass it first time and this means that the stigma attached to a failure will be that much greater than in the practical examination.

A second point to bear in mind is this: the failed theory candidate has no one to hide behind. There is no evil-eyed examiner to blame, no offending road-users, no alleged quota system of success. All of the candidate's friends will have completed the same examination. The only person that the candidate can blame is him- or herself.

Thirdly, it is quite feasible that many of the candidates who fail will already know how to drive after a fashion. They may have had road experience with trained drivers or illicit driving in their own right. The conviction that they know more than students who can pass an irrelevant theory examination will cause real frustration and anger.

The emotional response to a test failure can be split into three separate components:

1. *Resentment* is the first emotion that will register with an unsuccessful candidate. This may be expressed against 'the system', the course tutor or those who have passed the examination. The anger felt often takes the form of disappointment or tears, but is essentially self-criticism.
2. *Resistance* then follows. The student, in an attempt to block out an unpleasant memory or thought, will refuse to listen to advice and will throw up mental barricades.
3. *Rejection* is the final phase. It is at this point that the student may look for alternative tuition or may give up altogether on the idea of driving. Alternatively, they may just give up on the idea of getting a licence and drive illegally.

Whichever system of tuition you have opted for, be it theory first or theory and practical combined, it is vital that you get to know the test results as soon as possible. Ask students to contact you the minute they know their results or perhaps ring them yourself. You need to be able to counsel or console students who have failed before destructive self-criticism sets in. On a more practical note, you may have to resell the benefits of training or isolate especially demotivated students from the rest of the group. If combined training is involved, you will need to deal with the negative effects of failure before you advise on further practical training.

During your enquiry, try to listen more than you talk. It is essential that the student is allowed to express his or her feelings and what they say may well provide you with clues as to what should be done next. You must also inspire them, of course, and let them know that you may have a solution. Set aside time for a meeting where you can talk on a one-to-one basis.

REASSESSMENT

Before you can take any remedial action with a demotivated student you need to carry out a diagnosis. This is best done in the form of a reassessment in which you will go over many of the questions you asked in your initial fact-find. Go through the following points again, spending a bit longer on each of them than you did in the first instance:

- Has the student a learning disability such as dyslexia? Like students with the next problem, sufferers quickly become adept at covering it up. Check that they have not slipped through your net by discreetly getting them to read aloud to you.
- Has the student got a literacy problem? Again, it is possible that they somehow managed to fool you. Illiterate people are certainly not stupid. They may well have used something like a lottery technique on the multiple-choice questions rather than shame themselves. Ask them to read aloud to you or give them a test paper to read back to you, but be discreet. If there is a problem, deal with it sympathetically.

- Does the student have an underlying physical condition that could be responsible – for example, low blood sugar linked to stress which is common among diabetics. If, during your questioning, the student mentions any health problems, urge them to see a doctor.
- Is the student actually reading texts and hand-outs, or just telling you that he or she is? You need to be fairly direct about this.
- Does the student have a quiet place to study? If not, can you recommend one, such as the local library?
- Is the student making use of approved material or is he or she getting 'good' advice from someone else?
- Does the student need help in diary control to set aside study time?

If you have gone through the above checklist and found out the root cause of the student's problem, then the action that you need to take may be self-evident. If nothing has come to light, however, then more radical treatment is required if you want to help and keep him or her as a paying customer.

ALTERNATIVE APPROACHES

There is no point telling a demotivated student who has failed the Theory Test several times to 'study harder'. This approach has let them down to date and will most likely do so again. If the student is suffering from pre-examination nerves, peer pressure or depression, then these factors must be dealt with before learning can proceed. You need to treat the illness not the symptoms, the cause and not the effect. To do this you may have to recommend some strange actions. However, as long as both you and the student believe that what you are doing works, then it most probably will. In medicine, this is called the 'placebo effect'. The wonder pill prescribed may be nothing more than sugar, but the conviction that it can achieve miracles often has the desired effect in imaginary conditions.

THE GOALS SCRAPBOOK

Rewards and treats were served to motivate your students when they were young, and the same principle holds true for them in adult life. As small rewards are earned through good performance, both the conscious and subconscious mind become accustomed to success, that the prize to be won is worth a little discomfort. When this happens, examinations become a source of excitement rather than of worry. Instead of paralysing fear, there is the excitement of a challenge and the surge of adrenalin that will help the student over the final hurdle of self-doubt.

Ask your students to buy a cheap scrapbook, the kind they may not have owned since childhood. Then ask them to list four or five material items they really want. These should not be overly expensive; the aim is to develop attainable goals in every sense. Channel them into thinking about items like CDs, books, ties, etc. Whatever they are, they must be *really* desired.

Students are then asked to search through magazines, papers or catalogues for pictures of the items on their list. These are cut out and stuck into the scrapbook, one item to a page. The final step is to link each of them to a specific target – a percentage score in a mock examination, for example. As soon as the student has attained the target, he or she is entitled to go out and buy their reward, which they can then 'present' to themselves.

During the training process the goals scrapbook needs to be flipped through at least once a day. As a further inducement, the book can also contain a picture of the kind of car they are most likely to drive when their training is finished. This procedure can then be repeated as they move towards the practical driving test.

ANOTHER MAGNIFICENT SEVEN

The power of films to inspire, enthuse and change behaviour patterns is accepted everywhere but in the training field. Yet, used correctly, popular films can take demotivated students through many a sticky patch.

Ask your students to name their seven favourite films. These could be comedies, romance, Westerns, cartoons – in short, anything that leaves them feeling bigger and better for having watched them. Get them to hire videos of their selection and to play one a night on the seven days leading up to their test date.

The individuals using this technique which seems unrelated to any study methods are feeding, in actual fact, their subconscious minds with self-selected inspirations that you, as their tutor, could not hope to guess. As a final motivator, encourage them to whistle or hum the theme tunes of their favourite films as they wait to go into the examination room. As soon as they do so, the good feelings and memories associated with the music will rush back and banish any pre-test fears they may be suffering.

AFFIRMATION CARDS

These simple but effective devices work on two time-honoured axioms. The first is that 'seeing is believing'. The second is that if you say something often enough, you come to accept that it is so, whether or not it actually is.

Give your demotivated students a sheet of paper and 21 index cards. (These are very cheap, so you can afford to be generous.) Ask the students to write down short sentences that confirm the benefits that passing the Theory Test will bring them. These could be something like 'When I pass the Theory Test I can concentrate on my driving' or 'When I pass the Theory Test I'm going to have *such* a night out!' They could also add sentences such as 'Reading these lines will help me pass the test!' It does not matter too much what the sentences are, as long as they are important to the individual student. Encourage them to apply some real thought to this seemingly useless exercise.

The next step is to transfer these inspiring sentences to the cards you have provided. Get the students to write in capital letters in vibrant, positive colours – the ones that they prefer above all others. An alternative for those who have access to typewriters or word processors is to create labels which can be stuck on to the cards. This makes the messages look even more believable and impressive.

The finished cards should then be placed in an envelope or wallet to keep them clean. Any which become tatty or torn should be replaced at once. The student must then read a minimum of seven times daily all the way up to the Theory Test. This can be done in spare moments during the day at work, at home or before going to bed. (Try to use the numbers suggested. They are 'magical' numbers, and even in our hi-tech society, our culture and behaviour sees them as important or lucky.)

By reading these feel-good messages so often, the student will come gradually to accept them. They will permeate through the conscious into the subconscious mind, where they will push aside and replace the negative thoughts that have built up around the Theory Test.

LETTERS TO RELEASE FEELINGS

Many students, especially the younger ones, will suffer considerable peer pressure, as mentioned earlier. The majority of the people they know will have passed their Theory Test at the first attempt and this, of course, will be a constant source of 'extraction of the urine', as it has come to be called. The demotivated student alone is not going to see the funny side of the situation, so you should help him or her by supplying a way in which they can express their anger.

Ask the student to picture for a few moments the three people who are causing them the most problem with regard to their inability to pass the Theory Test. Ask them further to think of what they would like to say to those people, no matter how sarcastic or rude, on getting through.

Tell your demotivated student(s) to write down these words in the form of a letter they are never going to send. As they relax and laugh on hearing this, encourage them to pour their feelings out on paper. At this point, give them an envelope and tell them to seal it up. (For safety's sake, write 'do not post' on this and get them to give it to you. When they pass their test, you can return it to them to laugh over or to tear up ceremonially.)

For those of you whose students are too genteel to contemplate such thoughts and whose friends are so supportive that they will not laugh, try a different tack. Get them to buy funny postcards on which they should write 'I've passed!' or some such phrase. These should be dated for the next sitting and sent off or retained according to the individual's courage.

POST-DATED CHEQUES

A simple motivator is for the student to write out a post-dated cheque to him- or herself. This should be for an amount of money which can be spent on passing the examination. For best effect, it needs to be pinned to the main study book or work-sheet.

HYPNOTHERAPY AND OTHER ALTERNATIVE PRACTICES

A few students will be so deeply upset by their failure and worries that nothing you do for them will seem to help. If, having doubled-checked for all the possible contributory factors mentioned at the beginning of this section, you can find no solution, then alternative methods should perhaps be considered. Some of these practices may seem unusual, but they do offer a ray of hope. When a student is physically sick prior to examinations or loses sleep or their appetite, then they need help wherever it may come from. Regardless of your own attitude to these options, you should at least be aware of them, even if only to steer your students away from the more obvious charlatans.

Hypnotherapy enjoys a good reputation for helping people to overcome their phobias or anxieties. The mechanics of the process are still not fully understood, but essentially the subject is put in a state of altered consciousness where fear is suppressed. This can lead to very remarkable results, such as people with a lifelong fear of heights overcoming it with a bungee jump!

It is important to realise, however, what hypnotherapy *cannot* do. No form of hypnosis can make a person remember information that he or she has never seen, nor can it make someone a capable driver without previous study. What it offers is a method of preventing fear from disrupting performance, and in this sense it is worth taking note of.

Aromatherapy, as its name suggests, works through the effect of scent on our sense of smell. Although, as animals, we have evolved away from this sense in favour of sight, a familiar odour or scent can still have a profound effect on our moods. A lingering perfume can bring back happy or sad feelings, a long-lost smell from our childhood days can plunge us deep into reverie; a gust of wind on a rain-freshened morning can make us feel alive and at one with creation. The power of smell on our senses should not be underestimated.

The practitioners of aromatherapy claim that the application of various oils can be used to control our entire mind/body systems. Some of the claims made for it are a little hard to believe, but, like so many things, if it is believed to work, it will work. Students are best left to seek out a trained aromatherapist if they want to explore fully this discipline, but a related exercise can be sensibly worked into training.

Ask students to buy their favourite new perfume or aftershave. It has to be a new one, free of associations. Encourage them to spend some unhurried time in a large store until they find one they really like.

With their choice to hand, the student should then set ten

minutes aside each day. Relaxing music that also needs to be chosen with care is played as they sit and think about the things in life that make them feel good – relationships, holidays, etc. Somewhere into this sequence they should hold a mental image of themselves passing their Theory Test. While they are visualising this, they can smell the scent from their cherished bottle. The scent should *not* be put on at this stage, however. Once the exercise is over, the bottle should be stoppered and put away.

The above process needs to be repeated every day up to the test. Then, and then only, should the student wear their favourite perfume, and all those good memories and feelings associated with it should come flooding back. As pulses race and hearts pound in the seconds before the examination, they should let the smell take them back to the tranquil mood they have created around it.

Medication is often sought by candidates before they take their practical driving test, and the theory examination will prompt exactly the same response from those who believe that there is a miracle pill for every problem. Every ADI will have encountered students who have acquired drugs by prescription which they have wheedled out of doctors or 'safe' herbal remedies bought over the counter. The use of such chemical confidence is to be widely deplored and students should be advised against it as it can lead to the abuse of other substances in the belief that it worked the last time.

Acupuncture might seem a little impractical, but a form of it can be safely used by the student prior to an examination. This form is acupressure where pressure from the finger is used instead of a needle. The human body is studded with nerve clusters and other energy spots which are exploited, in a different method, by martial artists. Acupressure utilises many of these points for gentler reasons. Whether you believe that the effect is produced by the manipulation of the body's energies or by the release of nature's pain-killers, endorphins, it does work. And even if it does not, anxious students can use the technique to convince themselves that they are in control.

The energy points to be utilised, conveniently enough, are situated on the hands and their use should not cause any undue attention (see below).

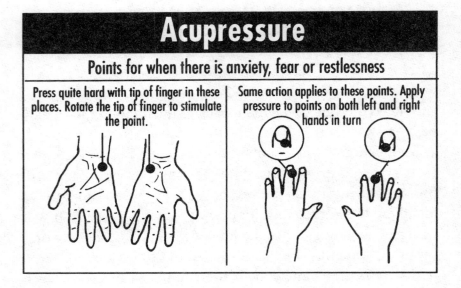

Acupressure

Points for when there is anxiety, fear or restlessness

Press quite hard with tip of finger in these places. Rotate the tip of finger to stimulate the point.	Same action applies to these points. Apply pressure to points on both left and right hands in turn

Once the point is found, the student should press his or her other finger on it deeply and firmly. The finger should be held at right angles to the flesh. The pressing finger should be rotated in a circular way and the pressure maintained for one to three minutes. During this time the student should concentrate on the effect that this action will have and *believe* that it will work. He or she needs to affirm what they are doing by saying, for example, 'I am doing this to calm my nerves'.

The use of exercise in the weeks leading up to the test is also recommended. Such exercise can be hard and physical, with the intention of burning out stress, or a more gentle approach like yoga or Tai Chi can be sought. Obviously, the choice rests with the student and what is locally available. The benefit of such activity is as much mental as physical – it gives the student something else to worry about! Failed students may well wonder what sort of an ADI they have when they are being made to learn a new skill or train hard as well as having to study for the Theory Test. The answer, hopefully, is an effective one. In a multiple-failure situation, the student needs to be kept busy. Nine times out of ten you are not working on a lack of knowledge but a lack of self-confidence that produces panic or a mental shut-down.

All, some or none of the above methods can be incorporated into a training programme, as you desire. The more specialised techniques will require a skilled practitioner, of course, and these can be found in your telephone book. When you have established the capability and the credibility of such individuals, you can then build up a combined approach. At this point you can advertise specifically for multiple-test failures and so tap into a new market.

10
CONCLUSION AND BEGINNING

TOLD ...?

One of the commonest phrases used in sales and training is 'Tell them what you are going to tell them, tell them, and then tell them what you have told them', and it is only fitting that this book should close on such a note. Besides, the central issues raised by theory training are so important that they are worth repeating a second time.

The first point made was that the provision of theory training is essential for the ADI in order to maintain pupil quantity, quality and respect. It is possible to dodge this unfamiliar method of working by any number of means, but in the end both the ADI and the pupil will suffer.

The second main topic raised was that the Theory Test can be used to bring about an irreversible change in public attitudes towards driving skills. By itself, the test cannot achieve this; if it is approached in an uninspired, dictatorial fashion, theory work will be as unwelcome and forgotten as schooldays' Latin, maths and so on. Taught correctly, however, it can affect students permanently. The ADI who follows this programme through will not only create safer drivers, he or she will create drivers who will be open to the idea of improving their skills for the rest of their lives.

Thirdly, and perhaps most contentiously, it was argued that driving instructors should cease to be instructors and become driving teachers. In both their own and the public's mind, ADIs need to make this subtle change in order to meet the challenges of the next century.

SOLD ...?

None of the above can happen without the active involvement of ADIs, of course. The changes demanded, though, in terms of practice and attitude will benefit everyone as the remainder of the chapter attempts to show.

SPECIALISATION AND NICHE MARKETING

The tropical rain forests of the world swarm with life, but nature there is not quite so red in claw and tooth as most people think. Jungles sustain a brilliant kaleidoscope of life not just because they are hot and steamy, but because their crowded inhabitants are not in direct competition with each other. Over millions and millions of years the animals in them have evolved in such a way that they all own their own special bit of habitat. If one animal feeds on the fruits and buds of a tree, another will crop the lower branches. Yet another will delight in tree bark, and some will eat nothing but roots. In this fashion numerous animals can coexist in a limited space. Each has found its own 'niche'.

Running a business is little different from surviving in a jungle. The relentless pressure to stay alive, the need for territory and the fear of competition all bear comparison in a very real sense. As in the wild, you can try to deal with competitors by being bigger, tougher or nastier, or you can avoid it altogether by specialising and finding your own place in the scheme of things.

Specialisation in theory can take several forms. For instance, you can develop your skills with reference to a particular section of the community – for example, older learners, younger learners, women-only groups, and so on. Some research will be necessary to get the most out of this approach. Learn the specific difficulties of your target group and what help is available to them from other sources in addition to yourself. Note and use any jargon or 'in' words they employ, what societies they can join and what journals they can read. Like moves with like, so polish up your referral techniques (see *The Driving Instructor's Guide to Effective Selling Skills*).

The other way in which you can establish a theory training niche is to offer a unique and exciting service to a more general audience. Study the list of potential topics in Appendix 1 and underline those which interest you. 'Brainstorm' each of these topics, writing down ideas or words that spring to mind. With a little effort you can turn these into day or weekend courses involving theory and practical work.

The exciting thing about most of these suggestions is that they can be sold to motorists at almost every stage of their driving lives. A day course on map-reading or fuel economy driving can be as useful to someone who has been on the road for ten years as it is to someone who has just started out.

The key word of the above paragraph is 'sold'. Optional extras of this type are going to require some active selling on your part. Follow the example set by other industries where the sale of increases or extras is a matter of course. Think for a moment about the financial adviser who every year visits you to increase your pension or life-cover, or the home-improvement company that returns some months after they completed the job for the other bit of work that you mentioned. These things may be sensible or desirable, but they would not happen without the involvement of a sales person.

Invent your 'product' and then try to sell it to previous customers. At first you may meet with resistance and difficulties, but persevere. The reward will be extra income and an inexhaustible supply of customers.

TRAINING FOR FREE!

It is possible to offer theory training for free and still make a profit in certain circumstances. The solution to this seeming paradox rests with an idea that nowadays is commonplace in almost every walk of life – sponsorship. Theory training, with its stated goal of preventing accidents and deaths, especially among younger drivers, is the sort of activity that organisations who have money to give away like to get involved in. A little spade-work is required to get a project like this going, but the rewards are considerable for all those involved. By working with one or more partners, the ADI can tap into a vast and unexpected market and achieve career satisfaction at the same time.

To begin with, you need to define the particular social group(s) that you feel need help with theory training and that you also feel you can really assist. Such groups can be narrow and specific – for example, inner-city youth, ethnic minorities or ex-offenders – or more general such as a village or neighbourhood. You need to be able to talk numbers in every case, however. Sponsors, like everyone else, will demand value for money.

Once you have defined your target audience, spend a little time in the library researching it. Getting in touch with relevant community organisations is also useful because they may well lend their names to your cause, as well as provide information.

The next step is to turn your findings into a brief report – that is, four to six pages of double-spaced type at the most. The sort of people at whom you are aiming this document will not have the time and patience to wade through a proposal the size of a small novel, no matter how worthy its cause! Besides, imagine your own reaction if you found a thick report that had to be read waiting on your doorstep. If sponsors want more information, they will ask for it. For the moment, you are trying to sell an idea and that is all.

The first page of your submission should use a bullet-point format. Underneath an exciting title, state your case and say as follows:

- Who you are trying to help.
- Why this group needs help with theory training.
- What the sponsoring organisation can hope to gain or achieve.
- Why you are the person for the job.
- All of the above wrapped in a final 'feel-good' line.

You should have no more than five or six bullet points on your opening page, and these should be well spaced so that the reader can focus on each in turn. The aim is to make a strong first impression; an over-crowded, fussy page will achieve the opposite. By the same token, a bullet point should be no longer than a single sentence.

When referring to yourself on this or other occasions, stick to the third person – for example:

■ Taught by a qualified instructor with 16 years' experience.

Still on the subject of yourself, include your name, address and telephone number on this page. A footnote at the bottom of the page looks very professional: 'Ann Instructor, Bewildered House, Anytown, 123 456'.

The next part of your proposal should be a snappy overview or introduction. Although longer than a bullet point this should not be over-long; a few straightforward paragraphs will suffice. Let the reader get used to the idea of reading. Think of a big meal that opens with a starter or an exercise session that commences with a warm-up.

If possible, keep the introduction on a separate page. Never be afraid of leaving a blank space as it shows the reader that you are not prepared to waste his or her time with useless information.

The next section needs to contain the most important points of your proposal. Even here, though, do not go overboard with facts and figures which are better placed in an appendix at the end. Let your argument flow smoothly and without distractions.

Then move on to a paragraph explaining why the sponsor will benefit from backing the scheme you are proposing. For a charity or a trust, this could be to fulfil its obligations; for a company it could be free publicity highlighting social awareness. Do not oversell this aspect. Let the reader generate his or her own excitement.

Next, you need to provide some information about yourself. As mentioned earlier, for best effect this needs to be described in the third person. It is more than likely that someone will be reading your proposal aloud to a committee or decision-maker, so help them out, for example, as follows:

Ann Driver has worked as a qualified driving instructor or ADI for over 16 years. In addition to this, she also holds a City & Guilds Adult Training Certificate and is fully trained in roadside first aid.

Ann's work frequently sees her involved with ethnic groups where segregation between men and women poses its own training problems. By designing this course exclusively for females to whom English is a second language, Ann hopes to be able to increase the mobility, job prospects and self-esteem of the ladies concerned.

In this, as in all the previous sections, be very careful to explain any jargon. Just because you happen to know what an ADI does for a living, it does not mean to say that everyone else does.

The conclusion that you offer is really a restatement of everything you have said but with added urgency, a reminder, perhaps, of how in-depth theory training can help to reduce the carnage on our roads.

To this, add any appendices stating relevant facts and figures, then staple everything together or slip it into a plastic wallet.

Now that you have an exciting, concise report what should you do with it? There are three main areas of potential sponsorship that you consider sending it to.

1. *Trust funds* have only one real objective in life, and that is to give away money to those who need it and who fit their criteria. There are literally hundreds of trusts and you need to select the appropriate ones in order to avoid wasting their time and yours. It is pointless, for example, to ask an organisation concerned with the Arts to sponsor a practical training course, and so on. Selection is best accomplished by reading through a current copy of *The Directory of Grant Making Trusts*, which is available in most reference libraries; this will also inspire you with

ideas as to how you can modify training in order to qualify for other grants.

2. *Government agencies* work on similar lines to the above, although in general they are less likely to make a quick decision. The funding made available by these can be quite significant, however, so they are well worth investigating.

3. *Business* offers another exciting field of potential sponsors. Petrol companies, insurance companies and car manufacturers could reasonably be approached with a view to sponsoring 'serious' theory work. At the opposite end of the scale are local shops or trade organisations who will also see this as a fair deal (their name will appear on your literature, they will receive credit in any media interviews, and so on).

With your list complete, you can now plan a mail-shot. Enclose the briefest of cover notes that offers just enough information to make the reader reach for the proposal itself. Keep a file of what you sent out and when, together with any responses.

Having sent out a proposal, forget about it. Committees and managers work to their own internal rhythms and, as you are asking for a favour, there is nothing you can do but accept this. When the replies do come, they may not be encouraging: 19 companies out of 20 may say 'No' to you; the 'Yes' that comes from the twentieth, together with a cheque, will make the effort seem worthwhile.

Involvement in sponsored training can provide an unexpected source of income, but that is far from the entire story. A deal with a company means that you can offer theory work as part of a life-skills approach not only to new drivers, but to drivers who have been on the road for 20 or 30 years. The scope and size of this market is limited only by your imagination and willingness to knock on doors and sell.

A STORY

There is a story that you might want to think about in connection with theory training. It goes like this:

A man was walking along the road one day when he came across a little boy who was standing crying in front of a barrel full of shiny red apples. At once he asked the youngster why he was so upset. The little boy sniffed and said that he would soon run out of apples, that he hadn't enough to eat.

The man was puzzled by this and pointed to the container overflowing with big, juicy apples. 'Yes', said the boy, 'but I'm only allowed to take one bite out of each, so they'll soon run out.' The man thought about this for a moment, then whispered that perhaps nobody would notice if he took two bites out of the apple instead of one. All at once, the boy was happy and dancing.

Are you willing to take more than one bite of the apple before you throw it away?

APPENDIX 1
LIFE-SKILLS TOPICS

The life-skills approach to driving tuition necessitates that the ADI has something to say to the motorist whatever his or her degree of attainment. This, of course, is exactly the case, but both the driving public and ADIs seem reluctant to grasp the nettle. Only by sowing the seeds for this attitude shift at the theory training stage can it ever come to fruition. The ADI should mention that he or she will be keeping in touch with past pupils for life from the moment of induction.

The following are just a few of the topics that can be offered as training sessions to qualified drivers or learners:

Choosing a car.
Buying and selling a used car.
Motorway driving.
Bad weather driving.
Night driving.
Basic maintenance.
Accident procedure.
Beating the car criminal.
Defensive driving and fuel economy.
Coping with road rage.
Safe driving for women.
Cold weather survival procedure.
Getting the best insurance deal.
Map reading and journey planning.

The list of subjects tackled is limited only by your imagination and skill. You must first hammer home this attitude during the preparation for the Theory Test, however.

APPENDIX 2
A SELECTION OF ROLE-PLAY SCENARIOS

WHO'S RIGHT?

Describe a not uncommon and very frustrating situation. For example, 5.30 on a busy weekday, a driver has come to collect his or her partner from work. This entails a short wait on the double yellow lines outside a department store, which is permissible, isn't it? The problem is that the chosen spot is also next to a bus-stop.

A bus comes along whose driver insists that in the interests of passenger safety he will only set down on the stop. He parks alongside the parked car and thus creates a tail-back. The car driver and the bus driver both claim that the other is unreasonable, but is that the real cause of the argument or is it just pride?

Use this role-play to examine attitudes and emotions rather than just who is in the right. As in so many driving situations, opinion can enter into situations. The point of the exercise is for students to understand what is really going on.

ACCIDENT!

The staging of a road accident provides an excellent source

of role-plays that can modify both attitudes and responses. Ideally, the role-play should follow immediately on from a case study or discussion about emergency procedure. Get one of the players to play the semi-conscious victim and another to act the dazed and upset driver. Other roles can be motorists, bystanders or friends of any of the above. The time is one minute after ground zero. Traffic has come to a stand-still, and no one is going anywhere. Reactions may range from hysteria to indifference. Inject a little panic into the situation yourself as necessary.

Make the debriefing a very thorough one. As well as going over again the proper drill and recovery positions, get the players to speak about how they felt.

ANOTHER LITTLE DRINK

Set this role-play in a restaurant. The group has had a nice meal and is about to break up, but someone suggests one for the road. A player selected by lot beforehand is the only person driving. The job of the others is to make him or her take a drink through whatever sarcastic comments, jokes and pleas they can think of.

Make the scene as realistic as possible by setting out chairs informally and providing soft drinks. The debriefing exercise needs also to cover what smart and face-saving answers could be used to counter peer group pressure.

Another role-play can be used in which the guilty driver has to tell parents, partners, police, friends, and so on what he or she has done.

GUILTY!

Alas, the non-drinking driver gave in to the taunts and jokes of the group. The result was a fatal accident which stole the life of a 17-year-old pedestrian who thought he was safe on the footpath.

Create a nightmarish trial. Don't get too hung up on realism – the aim is to explore emotions and consequences. The guilty driver is confronted in turn by parents, friends, police and even by the dead boy himself.

This can be a powerful, traumatic role-play. Your objective is not just to get the class to pay lip-service to the usual warnings, but to feel the full depth of the emotions involved.

APPENDIX 3
RECOMMENDED READING

The following works deal in much greater detail with subjects that have been mentioned in the text. It is strongly advised that any ADI working through a self-training programme consults all, or at least most of them.

How to Pass Any Exam
Brian Duncalf, Kyle Cathie, 1994

This book should be made compulsory reading for anyone who is involved in a teaching capacity, whatever their speciality or status. Written with warmth, enthusiasm and skill, it is packed with useful ideas. The 'dialogues' between author and student are particularly valuable – learn these well as you are likely to get involved in many of them! Essential reading.

Body Language: How to Read Others' Thoughts by their Gestures
Allan Pease, Sheldon Press, 1981

Few, if any, books on body language, are as good as this one. A comprehensive guide to gestures and stances, it will help you to understand both what your students are really thinking and what messages you are unconsciously sending them. Highly readable and highly recommended.

Unlimited Power
Anthony Robbins, Simon & Schuster, 1988

Like the preceding title, this book also has applications for yourself and your students. It is unlikely that most of your students will bother to read it, however, so do the work for them. A very helpful tool in judging how individuals learn and for helping them with motivational problems.

How to Master the Art of Selling
Tom Hopkins, Grafton, 1982

I make no apologies for including this now classic text in a book about teaching. As mentioned in the Foreword and elsewhere, as an ADI you are in competition with all sorts of people who want to teach theory. They may even be better than you, but are they as good at selling as you should be?

The Driving Instructor's Handbook
John Miller and Margaret Stacey, Kogan Page, 1993

Practical Teaching Skills for Driving Instructors
John Miller, Tony Scriven and Margaret Stacey, Kogan Page, Second Edition, 1995

Do not let familiarity with these two volumes breed contempt. Both have a great deal to offer you, perhaps even more now than during your own ADI training days. Regard each one as a gold mine that you can dig into for planning course work, structures and methods. If you have left them to gather dust, now is the time to pick them up again.

Instructional Techniques and Practice for Driving Instructors
L Walkin, Stanley Thornes Ltd, 1991 (revised edition)

Much the same can be said for this title as for the ones listed above. The new ground that the Theory Test has opened up calls for different teaching skills and attitudes; this book has a great deal to say about both and is recommended.

The Effective Use of Role Play: A Handbook for Teachers and Trainers
Morry van Ments, Kogan Page, 1989 (revised edition)

If role-play is to figure heavily in your training programme, then this work should be consulted. Examining the different kinds of role-play from both practical and theoretical standpoints, it provides more information than the average ADI is ever likely to use.

The Competent Trainer's Toolkit Series, 1–7
David G Reay, Kogan Page, 1994

The next best thing to a formal course in training methods! Each of the volumes in this series tackles a different aspect of the training process from start to finish. Valuable as both a self-development tool and in the design of course-work for students.

The First-Aid Manual
Andrew Marsden, Sir Cameron Moffat, Roy Scott, Dorling Kindersley, 1990 (revised edition)

As stated in the main body of the text, there is a real need for the ADI to be capable of dealing with an emergency both in the classroom and in the car. This comprehensive and easy-to-read guide forms the backbone of most official training courses and should be looked through at frequent intervals. It is an essential book, but one word of warning. It is *not* a substitute for proper hands-on experience. If you haven't already followed the recommendations made earlier and enrolled on a training course, then do so now.

Save a Life on the Road
Anon, Ebury Press, 1994

This is a simple but elegant idea. A micro-guide containing action cards, it comes in a plastic wallet to be fixed under the tax disc. In the event of an accident, the information and prompts that might be required are close to hand. Encourage your students to purchase one and, more to the point, show them how to use it!

INDEX

Index